GOVERNMENT
BY THE GUN

By the Authors

Robbie Robertson
The Contemporary Era: An Introductory History (1984)
The Making of the Modern World (1986)
Fiji: Shattered Coups (1988) (with Akosita Tamanisau)
Multiculturalism & Reconciliation in an Indulgent Republic: Fiji after the Coups, 1988–1998
(1998)

William Sutherland
The Pacific: Peace, Security and the Nuclear Issue (1988) (with R. Walker)
Law and Politics in Regional Co-operation: A Case Study of Fisheries Co-operation in the
South Pacific (1991) (with M. Tsamenyi)
Beyond the Politics of Race: An Alternative History of Fiji to 1992 (1992)

GOVERNMENT BY THE GUN:

THE UNFINISHED BUSINESS OF FIJI'S 2000 COUP

PLUTO PRESS AUSTRALIA

Z

First Published in 2001 by
Pluto Press Australia
Locked Bag 199
Annandale, NSW 2038
www.plutoaustralia.com

Published in Europe and the USA by Zed Books, 7 Cynthia St,
London, N1 9JF, UK and Room 400, 175 Fifth Avenue, New York, 10010, USA.
Distributed in the United States exclusively by Palgrave, a division
of St Martin's Press, LLC, 175 Fifth Avenue, New York, NY 10010, USA.

Cover design by Tracey Baglin
Copyedited by Bruce Pollock
Index by Olive Grove Indexing Services
Typeset by Bookhouse
Printed and bound by Hyde Park Press

Australian Cataloguing-in-Publication Data
Sutherland, William.
    Government by the gun : the unfinished business of Fiji's
    2000 coup.

    Includes index.
    ISBN 1 86403 139 5

    1. Fiji - Politics and government. 2. Fiji - Race
    relations. I. Robertson, Robert T. II. Title.

320.099611

UK Cataloguing-in-Publication Data
A catalogue record for this book is available from the British Library.
ISBN 1 84277 115 9 (PB)
        1 84277 114 0 (HB)

US Cataloguing-in-Publication Data is available from the Library of Congress

For assisting us in various ways during its writing,
this book is dedicated to
Akosita Tamanisau and Nemani Robertson, Helen Sutherland,
Sam Raman and Sue Oates, and Jim Sanday.

Contents

Glossary

ALTA	Agricultural Landlords and Tenants Act
BKV	Bai Kei Viti
CAMV	Conservative Alliance Matanitu Vanua
CCF	Citizens Constitutional Forum
CSR	Colonial Sugar Refining Company
CRC	Constitutional Review Commission
CRWU	Counter Revolutionary Warfare Unit
CUP	Citizens United Party
FAB	Fijian Affairs Board
FAP	Fijian Association Party
FDB	Fiji Development Bank
FHL	Fijian Holdings Limited
FLP	Fiji Labour Party
FNP	Fijian Nationalist Party
FPF	Fijian Political Forum
GEA	General Electors Association
GCC	Great Council of Chiefs

MFC   Moderate Fijian Coalition
NBF   National Bank of Fiji
NFP   National Federation Party
NPP   New National Party
NVTLP   Nationalist Vanua Taka Lovo Party
NLTB   Native Land Trust Board
NTFC   Nationalists' Taukei Civilian Forum
PANU   Party of National Unity
SDL   Soqosoqo Duavatani Lewenivanua
SVT   Soqosoqo ni Vakavulewa ni Taukei
UGP   United General Party
VKB   Vola ni Kawa Bula
VLV   Veitokani ni Lewenivanua Vakaristo Party

Chronology

PRE-COLONIAL

1200BC   First wave of 'Lapita' people populate Fiji.

100BC   Second wave of migrants, from Melanesia.

1000AD   Third wave of migrants, from Melanesia.

1800–1850 Early contact and trade with Europeans.

1830s   Predominance of Bau.

1847   The Tongan Ma'afu begins to control the Lau Islands.

1864–1911 Importation of 27,000 Pacific Island labourers.

1871–1873 Cakobau government.

COLONIAL

1874   Fiji ceded to the British by many chiefs. Fiji becomes a British colony. Arthur Gordon, first Governor of Fiji.

1876   Formation of Council of Chiefs, anti-colonial resistance in western and central Viti Levu suppressed.

1879–1921	60,000 indentured Indians imported to work in the sugar industry.
1882	CSR begins sugar production in Fiji.
1914–1946	Peasant resistance of Apolosi Ranawai and his Viti Kabani.
1944	Fijian administration reformed under the Fijian Affairs Board.
1959	Suva General Strike and riots.
1960	Cane farmer strike against CSR.
1966	Self-government introduced.

POST-INDEPENDENCE

1970	Fiji gains independence with Mara as first Prime Minister and a new Constitution.
1972	First general election. Alliance Party wins.
1973	CSR leaves Fiji.
1977	April election won by NFP but fails to form government. September election won by the Alliance.
1982	Alliance wins election.

1987

April	Election won by the Fiji Labour Party in coalition with NFP. Bavadra becomes Fiji's second Prime Minister.
14 May	Rabuka's first coup and establishment of an interim government.
25 September	Rabuka's second coup and formation of a military government.
7 October	Rabuka declares Fiji a Republic.
5 December	Mara heads a new interim regime. Ganilau becomes the first President.

1990	A new Constitution establishes the Sovereign Democratic Republic of Fiji.
1992	First elections since 1987. Rabuka becomes new Prime Minister with an SVT government.
1994	Mara becomes President.
1994–1999	Split in SVT forces another election in 1994. Rabuka returns as Prime Minister.
1997	New Constitution.
1999	May election won by the People's Coalition led by Chaudhry.

2000

19 May	CRWU attempted coup, led by Ligairi and Speight. Coalition members taken hostage, Suva looted.
23–25 May	GCC meets and endorses Mara as President.
27 May	Mara appoints Momoedonu acting Prime Minister. Momoedonu resigns and Mara assumes executive authority.
28 May	Ligairi's Dogs of War trash Fiji TV offices and shoot a policeman.
29 May	Mara steps aside as President. Army takes over and abrogates the Constitution.
4 July	Qarase appointed head of an interim government. Rebels seize the Army barracks in Labasa.
6 July	Rebels seize power-generating facilities at Monasavu.
8 July	Rebels seize Korovou town in Tailevu.
9 July	Army signs Muanikau Accord with rebels.
12 July	Speight holds his own meeting of chiefs, the Bose ni Turaga.
13 July	GCC meets and appoints Iloilo the new President.
14 July	Hostages released. Qarase announces his Blueprint for Fijian Development.
19 July	Rebels leave the parliamentary complex for Kalabu.
26 July	Speight arrested.

27 July	Rebels at Kalabu arrested.
28 July	Qarase's interim government reappointed.
2 November	CRWU mutiny, eight deaths.
15 November	High Court Justice Gates declares the interim government and the military abrogation of the Constitution illegal.

2001

1 March	Court of Appeal agrees with Gates decision.
8–13 March	GCC meets and reappoints Iloilo President.
14 March	Iloilo appoints Momoedonu Prime Minister and dissolves Parliament.
15 March	Momoedonu resigns and Qarase appointed caretaker Prime Minister until a general election under the 1997 Constitution in August.
1 April	Ravuvu Constitutional Review Committee reappointed. CCF launches a legal challenge against Iloilo's dissmissal of Parliament.
9 May	Qarase launches his new SDL party.
22 June	Qarase Government deregisters the CCF for engaging in political activities.
11 July	High Court rules that Iloilo's dismissal of Parliament and calling of fresh elections are justified by the Doctrine of Necessity.
19 July	Iloilo disbands the Constitutional Review Committee after the High Court (15 June) upholds an FLP writ seeking its dismissal.
25 August – 1 September	General Election.

Introduction

THE 2000 CRISIS

In the year 2000 Fiji experienced anarchy on a scale never before witnessed in the South Pacific nation. Not even during the military coups of 1987, Fiji's first taste of government by the gun, had arson and looting been so organised to terrorise the capital, Suva, where nearly one quarter of Fiji's 800,000 people live. But Suva did not suffer alone. Rebels occupied government premises across Fiji and seized control of the nation's power supply. Bands of thugs roamed the countryside with impunity to target defence-less Indian families. They destroyed property, stole possessions, food and livestock. They terrorised, beat and raped their way into the consciousness of people who never imagined such violence could be perpetrated against them. Thus Fiji acquired its first refugee camps as Indian farmers fled their homes, their lives in tatters.

But in this struggle there was always much more than met the eye. Fijians themselves did not escape the rebels' terror. Back in 1987, when Fiji experienced two military coups, brutality revealed itself largely as anti-Indian racism. In 2000 it had another dimension – a Fijian one. Fijians confronted Fijians on a scale of violence not seen since the early days of colonialism. Fijians killed Fijians. Commoners defied chiefs. Chiefs fought among themselves. Tensions between the country's 14 Fijian provinces ran high. Even the Fiji military suffered. Humiliated by its failure to contain the rebels, it had also to endure the shock of a violent mutiny. If nothing else, the unrest of 2000 shattered the myth of a united Fijian people.

WHY DID THIS HAPPEN?

The troubles exploded on Friday 19 May 2000 when a small group of army rebels and civilians, including their self-proclaimed leader, George Speight, seized Fiji's one-year-old People's Coalition Government. The rebels claimed that its Indian Prime Minister compromised the interests of indigenous Fijians. But the predominantly Fijian military refused to support the rebels and 10 days later seized control itself. To restore law and order and to secure the release of hostages held by the rebels, it tossed out the country's Constitution and established an interim government to oversee the drafting of a new Constitution. Then 70 days after the start of the crisis, it swooped down on the rebel base and arrested and detained its leaders.

But the army's belated decisiveness brought no peace. In November 2000 the army unit to which the rebels belonged mutinied. A short but bloody battle quickly suppressed the mutiny, but not before a new threat arose just as suddenly from an entirely different quarter.

The military argued that by seizing power on 29 May it wished to restore order and directly tackle the issues of indigenous dissatisfaction articulated by the rebels. Hence its abrogation of the Constitution and the appointment of an interim government. But at the beginning of March 2001, Fiji's Court of Appeal ruled those responses illegal. The military could not have its cake and eat it too. It could not claim legitimacy but act unconstitutionally. Yet another phase of political uncertainty began.

Given Fiji's history of coups, the attempted coup of May 2000 was not surprising. What was surprising were the reactions of the establishment — particularly the presidency, the military, the chiefs, and the judiciary. This time they displayed none of their former unity. Many of them undoubtedly supported the rebels' aims. Some claimed only to object to their methods.

Others looked askance at the increasingly radical direction the rebellion took and feared a commoner revolution.

This unexpected confusion was not simply the product of opportunism or the unforeseen, although these too were important elements. Behind these features lay deeper tensions whose origins go back to Fiji's colonial past. They have also to do with the development path Fiji has followed since independence, as well as Fiji's race relations, class interests and power struggles. Above all, they have to do with 1987.

Back in May of that year, Sitiveni Rabuka led a military coup. When Fiji's high chiefs challenged his goals, he staged a second coup. These coups and their consequences shaped Fiji's future in a way that no other event had done. They left a legacy of distrust, human rights abuse, corruption, and economic decline still fresh in the minds of Fiji's citizens in 2000. Yet the coups were also regarded by many Fijians as acts designed to protect Fijian interests and to strengthen the place of Fijians in Fiji.

Rabuka enshrined those interests in the 1990 and 1997 Constitutions, deepened Fijian political control, and enabled Fijians to dominate the public service. Indeed by some measures Fijians seemed to have gained the upper hand. By the end of the decade they dominated the country demographically. They accounted for 53 per cent of the population compared with 42 per cent for Indians and 5 per cent for others. And they owned more than 83 per cent of Fiji's land. An election in 1999 under a more democratic Constitution still produced a Fijian-dominated Parliament and a Fijian-dominated People's Coalition Government. Yet when Speight and his 'dogs of war' struck one year later it became immediately apparent that many Fijians still regarded themselves as disadvantaged. Why?

A major reason is the widely held perception that Fijians do not figure prominently in the country's economy, that they are economically disadvantaged. There is some substance to the perception. Rural areas in Fiji are most disadvantaged, and more Fijians live in rural areas than other peoples. But instead of grappling with disadvantage as an economic issue, many Fijians see it as a racial one. They compare 'Fijian economic failure' with 'Indian economic success'.

Of course, this perception does not equate with reality. Indians do not dominate the Fiji economy; transnational corporations do. Also, just as many Indians are trapped by poverty as are Fijians. But the Fijian perception of disadvantage persists and the envy it generates makes the management of cultural diversity in Fiji exceedingly difficult. Nonetheless, it does mean that the indigenous question is integrally tied to the broader racial one. The tragedy is that this history of racialism denies Fiji the opportunity to use cultural diversity to its advantage.

UNFINISHED BUSINESS

The central problem, then, is that after 30 years of Fijian political dominance, the aspirations of the majority of the Fijian people have not been realised. A small Fijian minority has done well, but not the bulk of the Fijian population. They feel neglected and isolated. They do not understand the nature of the economy they are part of, let alone understand how it is integrated into the global economy. Nor do they understand that many of the causes of Fijian disaffection lie within their own communities and institutions.

Instead of addressing these matters, Fiji's leaders have exploited the disadvantage of the Fijian masses by projecting it as the disadvantage of all Fijian people, the elites included. They have used the rhetoric of 'the paramountcy of Fijian interests' to hide the reality of the paramountcy of elite Fijian interests. The interests of the Fijian masses have always come a distant second. The 2000 crisis brought this contradiction into focus as never before. How to resolve it is the indigenous question. It is the key question facing Fiji today. It is Fiji's unfinished business.

OUR AIM

Our aim is to tell the story of what happened in Fiji in 2000, to uncover underlying causes and to draw lessons that might point the way to a more secure future for Fiji. We approach this task by focusing on the indigenous dimension because we believe that it lies at the heart of Fiji's problems. To better understand the indigenous question and why it is so difficult to resolve, we need to delve into Fiji's history, especially the history of the idea of Fijian paramountcy.

This will help us understand the complexity of the indigenous question. It will also enable us to better appreciate why recent attempts to push a Fijian nationalist agenda in the name of indigenous rights are so fraught with danger. The problem, we argue, does not lie in indigenous rights as such, but in equating indigenous rights with indigenous supremacy.

Our focus on the indigenous question does not mean that the concerns of Fiji's other communities are any less important, nor that those communities have a lesser role than Fijians in resolving the country's problems. Our view is simply that at the root of those problems lies the indigenous question, and until it is resolved there will be no real peace and progress. All Fijian citizens must be involved in resolving the country's many problems, including the indigenous question. But our view also is that in this task Fijians have a special responsibility. Why? Because many of the causes of the problems facing Fijians lie in Fijian communities and institutions; many of the solutions must therefore come from Fijians themselves. If they fail in this responsibility, the unresolved indigenous question will remain unfinished business and Fiji will go further down the road of government by the gun.

Chapter 1

Mayhem and mutiny – the 2000 crisis

OPPORTUNISM AND THE UNEXPECTED were notable features of the events that unfolded during Fiji's political crisis in 2000. But a closer probing of the situation reveal two more fundamentally important aspects: first, they were driven by deeper underlying tensions in Fiji; and second, as events unfolded the focus shifted from tensions between Fijians and Indians to divisions among Fijians. With the whole character of the crisis changing dramatically in this way, it became clear, as never before, that beneath Fiji's continuing problems lay a simmering Fijian issue that had been glossed over for a long time. Above all else, the crisis brought the unresolved indigenous question – Fiji's unfinished business – to a head.

INTRODUCING THE PLAYERS

The attempted coup on Friday 19 May 2000 drew heavily for inspiration on a similar coup in May 1987. But this new attempt had two striking features that set it apart: first, it was poorly planned and second, it stunned Fiji's main ruling institutions, which responded in confused ways.

The attempted coup was so poorly planned that it would have collapsed within one hour but for the improvisations of two very important recruits, former British SAS Warrant Officer Ilisoni Ligairi, and the man who became the very public face of the coup attempt, George Speight.

Ligairi had joined the British Army in the early 1960s and seen service in Ireland, Saudi Arabia, Kenya and Oman as a member of the Special Air Service. He retired to Fiji in 1984, where some three years later he became founding commander of the 70-man anti-terrorist Counter Revolutionary Warfare Unit (CRWU) established by Fiji's former strongman, Sitiveni Rabuka, as a palace guard to protect his 1987 coups. Regarded as a specialist elite, it trained apart from the rest of the army and jealously retained its guardianship ethos. The 60-year-old now Major Ligairi ensured that. Despite retiring in 1997, he remained extremely close to his 'boys' and they to him. Not surprising then that they turned to him to plan a simple repeat of Rabuka's May 1987 coup. He was still their commander in all but name.

At the eleventh hour the CRWU also drafted the media-savvy George Speight, a 44-year-old would-be-corporate star who had also spent most of his early life overseas, studying in the United States and working in Australia. His political and business connections in Fiji promised a privileged future after he returned in 1998. In little over a year he became one of the country's most senior forestry executives, poised to reap lucrative rewards from processing plantation mahogany. But that world crashed when the Rabuka-led government unexpectedly lost office in the May 1999 election.

These two men recast the CRWU coup attempt into a very different beast – a revolution that sent shock waves through the very community it purported to serve. Indigenous Fijians, these two men originally argued, were weary of marginalisation by Indians, one of whose sons – for the first time in Fiji's history – headed the country's new government. His departure from office was the coup's primary motive. But when the military failed to support the coup, they transformed it into a hostage crisis with the added goal of removing Fijian leaders whose preparedness to deal with Indians as equals had cost Fijians political leadership.

The second striking feature of this copy-cat coup attempt was the stunned and confused responses of Fiji's main ruling institutions; many members of these institutions were deeply involved in a year-long political campaign to oust the new Labour Prime Minister, Mahendra Chaudhry. In addition, the President, the Great Council of Chiefs, and the Fiji Military Forces, among others, were beneficiaries of the 1987 coups. Having acquiesced once, their hands were tied. 'We approve of the cause, but not the means,' they nervously intoned frequently.[1]

In May 1987 Rabuka had launched his coup to remove 'an Indian-dominated' Labour Government that had won office from the long-serving Ratu Sir Kamisese Mara just one month before. Mara rushed immediately to Rabuka's side and was restored, eventually, to the prime ministership. Thirteen years on, the 80-year-old Mara was halfway through his second five year term as President. Rabuka, the commoner who had succeeded him as Prime Minister for seven years until defeated by Chaudhry, now headed the Great Council of Chiefs. This supreme Fijian institution had also quickly endorsed Rabuka's coups in 1987. It even granted him life membership of the Council. In turn, a new Constitution in 1990 bestowed on the Council the power to appoint members of the Senate and to choose Fiji's president. L~~ ~~ewarded with a secretariat of its own. In addition, ~~ ~~ment company, Fijian Holdings Ltd, profited greatly ~~ ~~action policies.

~~ ~~nstitution, the military, also benefited from the ~~ ~~bled since 1987 and during most of the 1990s ~~ ~~ a blind eye to successive blow outs in the ~~ ~~members of one of its more highly politicised ~~ ~~nt with more than 34 hostages. Thus compro- ~~ ~~icult to resolve the situation decisively. It did ~~ ~~cordon it off. 'Let us not use the universal ~~ ~~o restore order', Rabuka advised. 'There ~~ ~~The army would think twice about going ~~ ~~ct decisively 10 days later, its interven- ~~ ~~would-be coup makers-turned-rebels to press their demands. Unexpectedly, the rebels rejected the army's all-Fijian nominees to an interim administration as 'has-beens', whose past failures had made their coup necessary.

Fijians were now confronting Fijians. Their leaders were not acting as part of a united political force. Mara and Rabuka had never trusted one another, and their differences now resurfaced.[3] Some provincial chiefs saw the attempted coup as an opportunity to redress long-perceived inequalities within the Fijian community; others saw it as an opportunity to consolidate a new and more radicalised Fijian leadership. Ligairi played to these divisions.

Hundreds of supporters had flocked to the Parliament to act as human shields should the army decide to attack. Now Ligairi organised them into fighting units. As his 'dogs of war' spread out from the capital to create havoc across the countryside, order became very fragile indeed. By threatening to stir the rumblings of commoners, Ligairi sent a strong message to all chiefs: commoners would take over if necessary.

George Speight played his part too, holding court in the parliamentary complex with his supporters and engaging with the international and local media. Unlike most politicians in Fiji, he was articulate and comfortable with the media–too comfortable, according to some journalists. They felt that their presence 'aided the rebel leader's propaganda fire . . . gave him political fuel'.[4] Some even wondered 'how much of the coup and its twists and turns was the product of the media itself',[5] especially when the military caved in and acceded to the rebels' demands. Speight and Ligairi emerged triumphant.

But the rebels had cost Fiji well in excess of $1 billion (equivalent to the government's total annual budget); $300 million in damage to infrastructure and lost government revenue alone. Over 10 per cent of the paid work force lost their jobs as the economy shrank an astonishing 12 per cent. In the tourist industry, occupancy rates plummeted 80 per cent, while Fiji's large garment industry lost nearly one quarter of its 20,000 workers. According to one estimate, 40 per cent more people now lived in poverty than when the crisis began.[6]

PAVING THE WAY: ANXIETIES AND DESTABILISATION PLOTS

Responsibility for the mayhem, however, does not lie solely with Speight and Ligairi. Ever since the May 1999 election there had been many conspiracies to topple the Chaudhry Government, although, as the President's private secretary Joseph Browne conceded, few of them anticipated a coup.[7] Among the conspirators were members of the Fijian establishment party, the Soqosoqo ni Vakavulewa ni Taukei (or SVT). Established by the Great Council of Chiefs, the SVT's share of the Fijian vote had collapsed from 66 per cent in 1992 to 34 per cent in 1999, leaving it with only eight seats in the 71-seat Parliament. Fijians still dominated the Parliament, but they were members of rival Fijian parties that joined Labour's People's Coalition Government as a demonstration of their opposition to the SVT. Thanks to the lack of proportionality in the country's new electoral system, Labour held a majority in its own right (37 seats).[8] Moreover, with the People's Coalition, it held just under two-thirds of Lower House seats. Never in Fiji had an establishment party been so devastated in an election.

The SVT's management board met immediately to discuss its future. One member urged Rabuka to lead another coup. He refused.[9] This time he would abide by the 1997 Constitution. This new Constitution, which Rabuka had done so much to put in place, obliged Chaudhry to offer the SVT at least three Cabinet seats. All parties with 10 per cent of the vote had that right, a right created under the Constitution to generate more inclusive governments and foster greater inter-communal cooperation. The SVT accepted the offer but demanded four specific Cabinet posts. Instead of negotiating, Chaudhry froze the SVT out. It proved a costly mistake. The inclusion of the SVT would have calmed the political climate. It would also have consolidated support for the new Constitution. By rejecting the SVT, Chaudhry made it easy for his opponents to resurrect the very politics of ethnicity the new Constitution sought to avoid. 'Chaudhry failed Fiji', Rabuka later declared. He 'had the mandate to bring this country together. He didn't. By his own style.'

But Rabuka was not without blame either. He refused to challenge Chaudhry's decision. Instead he declared the SVT the Opposition and 'retired' from politics to chair the Great Council of Chiefs. The man who succeeded him, Ratu Inoke Kubuabola, was not so accommodating. Indeed he was one of the founders of the Taukei (Fijian) Movement which had conspired with Rabuka in 1987.

When Kubuabola called his first SVT management board meeting, his response differed markedly from Rabuka's. According to former SVT adviser Jone Dakuvula, he angrily declared that 'people must be prepared to shed blood and die to get rid of the Chaudhry Government'.[10] Dakuvula believes that planning for a coup began from the moment in mid-1999 that Kubuabola linked up with disaffected members of rival Fijian parties within the People's Coalition, the Party of National Unity (PANU), the Veitokani ni Leweni Vanua Vakaristo Party (VLV), and the Fijian Association Party (FAP).

PANU was the creation of western chiefs and the mercurial Apisai Tora. During his long political career, Tora had been associated with most sides of politics, but his most enduring association had been with the Taukei Movement, which he had co-founded in 1987. Many PANU members hoped that the party would address western Fiji's long history of marginalisation by the east. It was a natural ally for the Fiji Labour Party which, under Chaudhry, had a strong following with Indian farmers in the country's west. But, as one *Daily Post* columnist argues, his coalition partner short-changed Tora. Labour cost Tora his seat by running a candidate against him. It also denied him a Senate seat and refused to rescue his ailing business. Consequently the People's Coalition paid 'heavily for its political faux pas and ... underestimating the power of an ageing but determined political nemesis'.[11]

Those Fijians disenchanted with Rabuka's abandonment of his 1987 goals formed the VLV. Strongly influenced by fundamentalists within the Methodist Church, they wanted Fiji declared a Christian state and Rabuka's 1987 Sunday Observance Decree reinstated. Not unnaturally, they made strange bedfellows for the Coalition Government, and were easy targets for Kubuabola in his quest for a Grand Fijian Alliance. So too were members of the FAP. They also collaborated with the Coalition because of their intense dislike of Rabuka. In addition, their western leader, Adi Kuini Vuikaba, the widow of Labour's 1987 Prime Minister, Dr Timoci Bavadra, had close associations with the Labour Party and had led it briefly after her husband's death. But with Rabuka gone and with members of the eastern province of Tailevu seeking to regain control of the party from Adi Kuini, the FAP rank and file were ripe for SVT overtures.

Nonetheless, the Grand Alliance failed to materialise. Talks between the SVT and VLV hit a snag in January 2000 when the VLV president demanded that the SVT first concede its error in not declaring Fiji a Christian state when it had the chance and for repealing the Sunday Ban in 1995.[12] In the FAP, the dissidents procrastinated.

The only thing that worked in Kubuabola's favour was the Coalition Government's appalling public relations. While Kubuabola struggled to undermine the Coalition's parliamentary support, he and his SVT colleagues were much more successful in whipping up popular fears that 'Chaudhry was cleverly pushing an Indian takeover and anti-Fijian agenda'.[13] Constitutional amendments which flowed from the new 1997 Constitution were presented as weakening Fijian institutions, even though they were, according to the First Parliamentary Counsel, substantially the same bills which the SVT had failed to put through during their final term.[14]

In the final analysis none of this mattered. What mattered was public perception. Almost from the start Chaudhry fell out with the media, especially the major English language daily, the *Fiji Times*. He tried to deny its expatriate editor-in-chief a work permit. When the *Fiji Times* responded critically to Government policies or published stories which showed individual ministers in poor light, Chaudhry overreacted and threatened to license the media to force 'more responsible' reporting. Some stories were overblown; some undoubtedly could be sourced to leaks emanating from SVT sympathisers. Part of the problem also resulted from the media being staffed by largely young and inexperienced reporters.

But inexperience was also a problem that faced this new Parliament. Much of the training of MPs undertaken in anticipation of multi-party government in the lead-up to the 1999 election had been lost because of its unexpected result. Rabuka's anticipated partners in government, the then largest Indian party – the National Federation Party – won no seats. Chaudhry also compounded the problem by making bad appointments. He made his son his personal secretary and a rookie politician his information deputy. Neither appointee had the skills or the temperament to woo the media, and both became the sujects of controversy themselves.

None of Chaudhry's issues with the press were intrinsically of great importance. But collectively they revealed an overly sensitive government unable to cope with even minor criticism as it 'tackled too many well-entrenched interests too quickly'.[15] It did not help that Labour had inherited a declining economy, with 30 per cent of its people living in poverty, 20 per cent of its children malnourished, and cities congested with more than 50,000 squatters.[16] Labour wanted to create a more caring state, to introduce a social wage with improved social services and infrastructure, and to halt the process of privatisation begun after the 1987 coups. It also wished to reverse the decline in rural infrastructure, to improve roads and upgrade educational facilities for all Fiji's citizens. Thirteen years after Bavadra, it still regarded itself as a multiracial party. Above all, it saw itself as a people's party, not a party for elites.

Although its goals were reformist, and not revolutionary, they were not always well received. Its attack on privatisation upset Fijian corporate interests who regarded privatisation as an important avenue for Fijianisation. Many commentators also cooled towards Labour's welfare measures. Its reduction of interest rates from 11 per cent to 6 per cent for low-income home buyers financially compromised the Housing Authority. The removal of consumption tax (VAT) from medicine and food probably advantaged the well-off more than the poor, and critics suggested instead better-targeted programs to assist the poor. Its attack on expatriates in the name of localisation simply created unnecessary diversions and achieved nothing.

Some changes did engender resentment. Labour axed Fiji's Intelligence Service and refused to renew Police Commissioner Isikia Savua's contract, extending his term by only two years. Mahogany development also created resentments. Some 52,000 hectares of rare plantation mahogany – variously valued at between $136 million and $500 million – would soon be ready for processing. Unlike the less valuable, fire-prone and poorer quality pine forests in western and northern Fiji, these high quality stands lay in Viti Levu's damp central and eastern provinces of Tailevu, Namosi and Naitisiri. Labour antagonised their chiefs by not consulting with them on the preferred partner for milling; more dangerously they upset a plan by some Fijian businessmen to profit from their links to one particular processing tenderer.

The controversies all these issues engendered, together with allegations about the misuse of ministerial entitlements and the treatment of some Fijians in the public service, began to take their toll politically. Labour had clear goals, but found it difficult to communicate them. Labour did poorly in municipal elections in late 1999. 'If we are not careful with the little things we're doing,' conceded Deputy Prime Minister Tupeni Baba, 'it will blow up in our faces.'[17]

In the end it was the land issue which most damaged the Coalition. Rabuka's Government had failed to resolve what would happen when some 40 per cent of the country's farm leases began expiring (one-third of these before 2005). Many Fijian landowners wanted their land back. They had expanding populations to accommodate or they wanted to farm themselves. Some believed that they did not benefit sufficiently from leasing land to warrant tying themselves to a new round of 30-year leases. If leases were to continue, they wanted them based on the market value of the land rather than its unimproved value, and the lease period reduced. Neither response addressed the issue of land degradation encouraged by short-term leases nor the difficulties Fijians faced obtaining loans for farm development. Such issues never had time to surface as the land debate degenerated into racial vilification.

The reason was simple. Land always involved more than landowner demands. It also involved thousands of tenant farmers, most of them Indian, who might at any time find themselves landless and unemployed. And it involved Fiji's collective economic welfare. Whatever happened to leases, Fiji had to ensure that it continued to earn vital foreign exchange from the productive use of its land. Any government would find these issues difficult to resolve. For this reason Mara, while endorsing Labour's Manifesto as good for Fijians, warned Chaudhry to give himself at least two years to win the confidence of Fijians before tackling the thorny issue of land.[18]

Labour proposed extending the 30-year farm leases and establishing a Land Use Commission with a broad brief to address, among other things, the poor state of rural infrastructure. The Native Land Trust Board (NLTB), through which all Fijian land is administered, bitterly objected to losing its monopoly. Its officials began a campaign at provincial and village levels to frustrate the Government's goals. They portrayed the Land Use Commission as 'a Trojan horse for a land grab and for emasculating the NLTB' and demanded that the board be privatised to remove it from government interference.[19] Labour had no effective answer to this. It met with NLTB officials to depoliticise the issue but with little success. They had a different agenda; in Dakuvula's words 'a scorched earth campaign against Chaudhry.'[20] Further, the Coalition's public relations efforts were focused almost exclusively on English print media, which it claimed was part of the destabilisation campaign.[21] Unfortunately for the Coalition, the land issue exploded at the same time as it introduced constitutional amendments. Both handed the SVT a new weapon to destroy the Coalition – a civil disobedience campaign against the changes proposed.

Pressure on the Coalition now assumed new forms. On 4 April in the western sugar capital Lautoka, Apisai Tora announced that he had reformed the Taukei Movement to organise Fijians to fight against the Coalition's land schemes and reforms. But its first rally in Lautoka on 20 April was disappointing. Only 300 people turned up. A rally in Suva eight days later was a very different affair. Eight thousand supporters flocked to the Civic Centre. This time members from a wider number of Fijian parties helped in the organisation, including FAP politician Ratu Timoci Silatolu as president of a new Indigenous Foundation. Tora's brother-in-law, Police Commissioner Isikia Savua, was alarmed. The Government needs to listen to the grievances of the Taukei Movement, he warned. The police may not be able to cope with more protest.[22] Chaudhry dismissed his concerns and told him not to interfere in politics.

At that very moment the previously insignificant Nationalist Vanua Taka Lovo Party (NVTLP) announced another rally in Suva on 19 May. The Indigenous Foundation and the Taukei Movement would assist it.

This sudden escalation in tension, together with the re-emergence of the Taukei Movement, sent shock waves through Fiji. Both the Australian High Commissioner and the US Ambassador urged Chaudhry to act cautiously. So too did many Labour sympathisers. It made more sense to create an atmosphere of stability and to address issues such as poverty and education than to pointlessly inflame ethnic tensions.[23]

But Chaudhry ploughed on regardless and his second deputy, Adi Kuini Vuikaba, came to his aid. 'Decisions of the nation's leaders should be respected,' she argued. Leaders should be left to implement what they thought was right.[24] Deputy Opposition leader David Pickering suggested an alternative solution: 'Replace Chaudhry with his deputy and do the whole country a favour.'[25] Some members of the Coalition came to the same conclusion. They were alarmed at Chaudhry's casual disregard of the dangers facing his Government. On 4 May Home Affairs Minister Joji Uluinakauvadra announced a ban on further protest marches but the next day Chaudhry overruled him. Coalition dissidents plotted his removal. He would be permitted to celebrate one year in office on 20 May but would be replaced by Deputy Prime Minister Tupeni Baba in the following week.[26]

Kubuabola also finalised an end game to his civil disobedience campaign. The SVT planned a motion of no confidence with FAP dissidents Silatolu and Ratu Tuki Cakanauto.[27] Whether an attempt to regenerate a Grand Fijian Alliance or, more simply, to prompt Coalition dissidents to move rapidly on their goal, we do not know. Kubuabola insisted that 'we were not interested in overthrowing a government that was selfdestructing'.[28] But no one, it seems, told Iliesa Duvuloco, the nationalist leader planning the protest march on 19 May. Allegedly he had a different game plan in mind.[29]

THE OPPORTUNISTIC COUP: NOT ACCORDING TO PLAN

Fiji's May 19 attempted coup did not however, originate with its Fijian politicians. That dubious honour went to the small Counter Revolutionary Warfare Unit,[30] half of whose members were away serving as peacekeepers in southern Lebanon and East Timor. It regularly kept in touch with its former commander and mentor, Ilisoni Ligairi. Indeed, it often trained in the Cakaudrove province on the northern island Vanua Levu where 'The Old Man' (*Na Qase*) lived on a small farm near his village outside Savusavu. They spent Good Friday (21 April) with him and during the next two weeks – in all likelihood – trained on Rabuka's 800 hectare Valavala estate, 73 km to the north-east. Certainly they met Rabuka briefly at Savusavu Airport when they arrived on 20 April (he was en route to Taveuni) and again three weeks later at a Sunday church service. A *yaqona* or kava session followed to commemorate his 14 May coup.

Such was the relationship between Rabuka and the CRWU that this was shared annually. Rabuka's departure from politics deeply disturbed the soldiers, and on this occasion they talked politics with him. They sounded him out about the demonstrations, 'how the Government was doing, how Fijian aspirations are being addressed or neglected by the Government of that time'. His advice to the soldiers and, he says, to anyone else who asked him then, was to 'apply as much pressure as we can'. He even considered marching himself at a later stage. But he always counselled against mob pressure and mob activity.[31]

Back in Suva two days later, 36-year-old CRWU Sergeant Vilimoni Tikotani had other ideas. Learning of Duvuloco's plans for a march the following Friday, he phoned a spokesperson for the NVTLP and offered Duvuloco a radically different outcome for his protest. It would be 1987 all over again. We do not know what conversations followed, but it is likely that some senior officials were sounded out to ascertain their reactions.[32]

But the more important point is the overriding ethos of the conspirators. This coup hinged entirely on one assumption, that the Fijian establishment would automatically rally behind the coup makers as it had 13 years before. Preparations, therefore, were rudimentary. The coup makers had simply to act as a catalyst for change and it did not matter that the plotters dealt mainly with players on the fringes of the Fijian establishment. Duvuloco's destabilisation committee allegedly included Tora, journalist Jo Nata, independent MP Simione Kaitani, and Silatolu, whose links with Telecom Fiji would be used to disrupt communications.[33]

Unknown at the time, one of the most vital links was with Duvuloco's relative George Speight, a man well-connected politically through his MP father, Sam Speight, and through his family friend, the millionaire MP Jim Ah Koy[34]. George Speight also regularly played golf with Rabuka. Despite these connections, Speight was also a fringe dweller, not known for any strong identification as a Fijian. Speight was not a 'pure Fijian'. Because his grandfather was European, he was treated as part-European. After the 1987 coups, when Fijian identity became much more important for access to resources and power, many people of so-called 'mixed race' controversially sought to be officially deemed Fijians. Speight's father was one of those, but such moves were not always well-regarded by Fijian conservatives.[35]

Thus Speight's role as the public face of the attempted coup contained a flaw which, in their hasty preparations, the coup plotters did not consider. Yet from the moment the hostage situation began, it became apparent. Journalists in Parliament that morning were astounded to see Speight among the rebels, and wearing a sulu (the Fijian formal sarong) for the first time. But for Speight, the sulu was part of the circuit breaker. His business ambitions had landed him in court. Currency exchange charges also loomed. On Wednesday 17 May he met the principal conspirators. They wanted his communication skills. Speight wanted to regain his future. 'Look, this is personal,' he later told journalists. 'Everything is personal when you're fighting for your race.'[36]

> Ligairi was now in Suva for a family funeral. The soldiers desperately needed his leadership, and authority. They felt out of their depth. 'When they told me the thing is set, I just asked, 'Who's this? Who's that?' And then I say, 'OK, go ahead.'37 But Ligairi's role was much more important than this sounds. In effect, he returned as their commanding officer, and his first task was to rally the army behind them.

Beyond that, the planning remained fragmentary and basic. 'There were not enough plans,' conceded Colonel Metuisela Mua, the former intelligence chief sacked by Chaudhry. 'Their commanding officer did his best to try and adjust and readjust the plans to at least what they wanted on the 19th.'[38] Over the remaining days they smuggled out weapons from the CRWU armoury. So far only six CRWU soldiers were involved. Three more were hastily briefed on the Friday morning. But the wider group now involved in the conspiracy only got together for the first time when they all met up at the Parliament on 19 May. Speight reflected:

> The story behind how the coup took place and how we met – all the players – is quite miraculous in and of itself. It's nothing short of providential influ-ence. And yet, I'm not a religious man. I haven't been to church in 15 years. And yet having said that, I think all of us in our hearts, you know, have a quiet resolve and respect for the Almighty, in our own way, but so, it'll shock you to learn that I met Major Ligairi on the morning of the coup for the very first time.[39]

In fact Speight was under the impression that he would meet several more players other than Ligairi. The nature of this conspiracy generated its own confusion.

By 10.00 a.m. on Friday 19 May Duvuloco's protest march was on its way to deliver to the President a petition calling for Chaudhry's removal. Five thousand noisy protesters waved banners declaring the 'Taukei Movement on the March' and 'Fiji for Fijians'. The police had a strong presence, but did not place its riot unit on standby.[40] 'Everyone in Fiji knew that the Taukei Movement was marching through Suva that morning, but no one had a feeling of what was going to happen,' a university student journalist recalled.[41] But the heightened police presence worried the conspirators. They were on edge. Ligairi's frontline team waited outside the city in a red four-wheel-drive and a minibus for a signal from Parliament that Chaudhry had arrived. At the last moment one of the late recruits, Captain Shane Stevens, deserted them.[42] To make matters worse, Parliament's 10.30 start was delayed. Once the signal came from Parliament, Ligairi went to rally support from the military. The vehicles headed for the parliamentary complex at Veiuto, an inner suburb of Suva. They nearly didn't make it.

As they impatiently sped their way through Suva's winding streets, two police cars gave chase. The minibus was stopped; its driver charged for speeding and overloading. But the four-wheel-drive continued, followed by a second police vehicle. At the entrance to the parliamentary complex, an officer witnessed the chase and began to close the iron gates. But not quickly enough. Within minutes the armed men were in the compound, their weapons out. The police backed off. As Speight's group rushed into the parliamentary chamber at 11.00 a.m., the second group rounded up staff and parliamentarians in various offices.[43] Chaudhry and Baba were hand-cuffed and dragged to the front of the chamber; their Coalition partners separated into Fijian and Indian groups and placed in different rooms. Opposition members were not detained.

Up at the Queen Elizabeth Military Barracks in Nabua, Ligairi ran into problems. If he thought that the absence of the military commander, Commodore Ratu Josaia Voreqe (Frank) Bainimarama, at a UN conference in Oslo increased his chances 'to muscle support', he soon found other-wise. Ligairi knew that many officers resented Bainimarama's appointment in 1999. A naval officer heading a predominantly army establishment had not won universal support. Ligairi attempted to use these tensions to his advantage. He was even given an opportunity to present his case, but senior officers, including Lieutenant Colonel Viliame Seruvakula, the commanding officer of Fiji's largest regiment, the 1400-strong Third Fiji Infantry Regiment, 'ordered their men not to be a party to the coup'.[44] However, despite this firm and unexpected rejection by the military, Rabuka believes that additional weapons were smuggled out that morning. 'At the time the perception was that Ligairi and the boys in Parliament were to be given more arms and ammunition to protect the hostages from the supporters of George Speight who had at that time crowded into Parliament.'[45]

Speight was not immediately aware of Ligairi's problems. After tying up his hostages, he indicated that he was waiting for the leader of the coup and others to arrive. 'People very high up, well known to us,' he declared. 'You will be surprised.' Poseci Bune, leader of the VLV and the man who had sacked Speight from his Fiji Pine directorship, remembers the moment well.

We had to wait about forty minutes as he was answering calls, and at the
same time making calls, telling us that we would be surprised that he is
not the leader, as the real leader would arrive for us to see him. But then
he got another call. Then he turned to us and said, 'I think he is going to
be late. Well, I'll have to take over from here.'[46]

The identity of the leader who failed to show up has never been made
public, although the press has since speculated that he was none other than
Police Commissioner Savua who, they allege, pulled out when he learned
that the military did not support the coup.[47]

　According to Bune, the rebels next turned to Rabuka to help them.
They wanted Rabuka as the new President. But a second surprise now
awaited the conspirators. Shortly before mid day, Rabuka arrived at the
parliamentary complex in response to a call from Speight, but he came not
as Speight's saviour but as a mediator. 'I sympathise with your cause but I
don't agree with your methods,' he told Speight.

　Rabuka had good cause to be wary of Speight and the CRWU rebels.
Knowing them personally placed him in a very awkward position. Indeed,
Mara accused him of being part of the plot but publicly at least backed him
as a 'trusted and invaluable mediator'.[48] But there was little trust between
the two men. Old antipathies had been stirred only weeks before when
Rabuka's new biography revealed publicly for the first time that Mara had
given the nod to Rabuka in the days preceding his 1987 coup. Rabuka now
also blamed Mara for his electoral defeat in 1999.[49] This was a very political biography; Rabuka had both a reputation and a career to recover and
he knew that one day soon the presidency would become vacant.

　During early negotiations with the rebels, Mara indicated that he might
ask Chaudhry to step down as Prime Minister and replace him with one
of his Fijian ministers. The rebels considered the proposal, but demanded
first that Mara also resign. Rabuka put this to him. 'You have just cele-
brated your eightieth birthday, you have had a very good innings.'[50] Not
surprisingly, Mara dumped Rabuka as his mediator and appointed legal academic Michael Kidd instead. The move proved disastrous. Speight ridiculed

Mara: 'Why should I talk to a white guy about the concerns of the indigenous people of Fiji?'[51] Mara was now under intense pressure. On Monday
22 May, Chief Justice Sir Timoci Tuivaga and two judges reportedly advised
him to dump Chaudhry and grant Speight an amnesty. That evening Mara
told the media: 'I can't say that I will put back the government that caused
all these problems.'[52] Whether intended or not, the concession sent a welcome
signal to the rebels.

Rabuka was also under pressure. As the Commonwealth special mediator in the ongoing Solomon Islands crisis, Rabuka desperately wanted to
enhance his future employment prospects by playing a statesman-like role.
Consequently he needed to distance himself as much as possible from Speight
and the CRWU team. Thus he quickly condemned the coup attempt, publicly
mocked Speight, and contrasted Speight's actions with his own in 1987.

> George Speight claims to be the champion of indigenous rights as I claimed
> in 1987. I am still waiting for him to make his announcement in Fijian . . .
> Why are they still in Parliament? Why don't they come out and take over
> their offices . . . map out what they are going to be doing and govern rather
> than holing up in Parliament with a whole lot of hostages?[53]

But Rabuka needed also to demonstrate decisive action. He wanted to test
Mara's support by calling a meeting of the Great Council of Chiefs for
Tuesday 23 May to resolve the crisis.

From day one, Rabuka's unexpected reaction threw the coup makers
into confusion. They had anticipated that he would join them. Consequently
they had quickly to rethink their strategy. Above all, they had to buy time.
One nationalist justified the events that followed: 'You had to have looting.
They didn't have an army, so they wanted to stretch out the forces, the
police forces particularly.'[54] At 1.00 p.m. the central business district of
Suva erupted into a $30 million orgy of violence and looting. Thousands
fled the city centre as shops were set on fire. Copycat acts of violence
occurred elsewhere around Fiji as well.

That evening President Mara declared a state of emergency and imposed
a curfew. 'What happened will be remembered as a day of shame,' he told

the nation. What horrified him most were the images of ordinary people rioting. Television pictures showed whole families picking through the remains of shops, children running off with baskets full of stolen goods. 'This is not the first time we have followed the road embarked upon by Mr Speight and his group of supporters,' he reflected. 'We went down a similar road in 1987 and it led us nowhere. Armed intervention and attempted coups are not the way to reach political and economic goals.' Speight dismissed Mara as out of touch. 'The President should listen to the wishes of the indigenous Fijians,' he declared.[55]

The rebels were disappointed with the reactions of the President and the military. They were particularly disappointed with the former Fijian Prime Minister, Rabuka, and were uncertain about the chiefs he chaired. Nonetheless, the confusion and indecisiveness shown by these pillars of the state and the Fijian establishment gave comfort to the rebels. As never before, Fijian commoners now felt emboldened to take on the authority of the state and the chiefs.

CONFRONTING THE PRESIDENT

The rebels knew that a higher level of visible support would help their cause and therefore wanted more sympathisers to join them in the parliamentary complex.[56] The President issued orders against this, but the rebels won out when, over a few days after 19 May, police allowed some 300 supporters or sympathisers to enter the complex. The failed coup now assumed new proportions.

At the start of the coup attempt, observers noted the confusion the rebels displayed when prominent politicians like Tora and Kubuabola refused to publicly endorse their actions. According to the *Review*'s Tomasi Digitaki:

> The selection and the swearing in ceremony of Cabinet members [seemed] poorly organised. In the middle of the ceremony we were told that there would be a break because some of the names of the Ministers were wrongly

printed. We later found out that those people had turned down the offer of ministerial posts.

To add to their woes, Bainimarama was now back in the country, and the rebels feared that he might try to storm the parliamentary complex.[57] Ligairi and Bainimarama spoke briefly to each other, but their phone conversation did not go well. When Bainimarama condemned his behaviour, Ligairi retorted that he should no longer regard himself as a Fijian.[58] Nothing, it seemed, turned out as anticipated. Digitaki noted:

> The hostage takers seemed disorganised. Each time a rumour surfaced of an army attack, some of the gunmen panicked. They would herd us into one of the offices and run around, switching lights off. We were terrified, yes, but from the look on their faces, we knew they were too.[59]

On the Monday, during one such panic attack, the guards dragged Chaudhry on to the lawn and placed a gun to his head. The pressure unhinged one guard; the rebels tried to hand him over to police but they refused to take him. Even Sergeant Tikotani waved his handgun erratically at reporters, and warned that the hostages would be shot if necessary.[60] Ligairi had his hands full maintaining order.

But the movement of supporters into the complex and the obvious differences between Mara and Rabuka encouraged Speight. So too did the messages of support from many chiefs.[61] Emboldened, Speight released nine MPs who had resigned under duress. Chaudhry's bodyguards were also released. Two more MPs were released the next day. But 32 hostages remained.

When Mara ordered the growing contingent of foreign journalists to move back one kilometre from the complex, Speight opened the door to them, even driving to a police checkpoint to secure their passage. He returned on foot in conversation with Assistant Police Commissioner Jahir Khan.[62] Digitaki later reflected:

> It was when the overseas press and members of the public were allowed inside the complex that we noted a huge surge in confidence in the hostage

takers. Speight, especially, thrived on the attention. It was quite obvious that he was using the media to popularise his group's coup.[63]

On the Monday Speight drove out of the parliamentary complex for a tour of devastated downtown Suva. No one arrested him. He told journalists that his new Parliament would house only Fijians. Other races might only observe. After all, the differences between them are immutable, he claimed. 'They have their own religion; they don't dress the same; they don't speak the same language.' And he spat, 'They don't smell the same.'[64]

Speight now declared himself head of state (the Taukei Civilian Takeover Leader) and made Silatolu his interim Prime Minister. Without consultation, he designated Colonel Ulaiasi Vatu the new FMF Commander and Colonel Filipo Tarakinikini his Chief of Staff. In addition, Speight announced the 1997 Constitution dead, abrogated in the name of indigenous rights by what he now called a 'Taukei Civilian Coup'.

Mara insisted that he had the support of the Great Council of Chiefs; in fact it was highly qualified. When they met on 23 May, they wanted to capitulate to Speight. But they also found it difficult to totally disregard Mara and Rabuka. Indeed Rabuka claimed to hold them back, insisting that the country's future depended on 'a kind of constitutionality'. But at the end of the meeting, he was forced to qualify his position: 'Democracy, we have always stated, [is] a foreign flower', and should be subject to amendments to suit local circumstances.[65] This return to the rhetoric of 1987 did not sit well with the remade statesman. In the past he had never apologised for his coups; now he found comparisons between this coup and his own difficult to stomach. 'It is unfortunate, but . . . the present [coup], just as mine, can probably never be justified,' he admitted days later.[66]

As for Mara, the chiefs endorsed him as President. They retained the 1997 Constitution but agreed to amend it to 'embrace all concerns that have been expressed by the Taukei'. In the interim, an Advisory Council would assist the President to govern Fiji and oversee constitutional changes. All the rebels would be pardoned and the chiefs would nominate many of them for inclusion on the Advisory Council.

But Speight was now in no mood for consensus. He immediately rejected the chiefs' compromise. He wanted the Constitution out and Mara with it. The Advisory Council sent a delegation to negotiate, but many of their number negotiated instead on their own behalf. New alliances were forged which would radically alter the direction of the CRWU coup and ultimately weaken its claims for universal Fijian appeal.

Over 1000 supporters now crowded into the parliamentary complex, and on Friday 26 May (Day 8 of the crisis) 18 territorial members of the Engineering Unit, led by Major Joseva Savua – the younger brother of Police Commissioner Savua – marched dramatically into the complex, pledging their support for the coup. Rumours circulated that Bainimarama permitted soldiers to choose. Other soldiers slipped in more quietly; and a campaign began to influence soldiers back at the army barracks to defect.[67] Certainly these were all positive signs for Speight, but he refused to commit himself to any deal until he got exactly what he wanted, including an amnesty. 'We want immunity from prosecution, like Rabuka got in 1987,' declared Kaitani. 'There is no other way', Speight mocked.[68]

To demonstrate his growing confidence, Speight and some 20 armed body-guards, followed by a media posse, strode out of Parliament on the Friday and confronted troops who had only just assumed responsibility from the ineffectual police for preventing access to the Parliament. The out-numbered troops backed off as Speight's supporters swept away their barbed wire barri-cade. But the next day a similar confrontation turned ugly as 10 soldiers reacted to the sudden presence of 200 rebels and supporters. Three soldiers and a rebel were hospitalised; one cameraman shot in the arm. It was an ominous sign of things to come. 'We understand their feelings', Bainimarama told journalists later, 'but not their methods'.[69] He withdrew troops from the checkpoints and replaced them with unarmed police officers.

Mara, meanwhile, attempted the impossible task of undertaking the chiefs' wishes legally. The Great Council of Chiefs possessed no constitu-tional authority to advise the President in such matters. Nonetheless, Mara decided to suspend Parliament and to employ a Council of Advisers to rule the country ahead of fresh elections. But first Chaudhry had to resign, which was unlikely. In any case, Speight denied the President access to Chaudhry.

Undeterred, Mara now deemed Chaudhry absent from duty and unable to perform the functions of his office. On Saturday 27 May (Day 9) he appointed as acting Prime Minister Ratu Tevita Momoedonu, a Minister of Labour in the Coalition, not present at Parliament on 19 May. On cue, Momoedonu advised Mara to dismiss his Cabinet and accept his resignation. Mara agreed, assumed executive authority, and declared his intention to appoint a caretaker government until elections could be held in six months time. But Mara made it quite clear that since Parliament had not been dissolved, his Council of Advisers could only include existing parliamentarians. It could not include Speight. He would consider granting the coup perpetrators immunity, but no negotiations could begin 'until freedom is granted to the parliamentarians and the people lay down their arms'.[70]

Speight angrily rejected Mara's solution. He should have done all that six months ago, he declared. For 30 years Mara had failed to make Fiji a nation and failed to listen to his people. 'If he had listened and acted on what Fijians wanted, this crisis would never have happened.'[71] But privately Speight seethed. He feared being outmanoeuvred by Mara. On Sunday his group struck back.

That evening on Fiji TV's *Close Up* program, reporter Sayed-Khaiyum interviewed Jone Dakuvula, now a member of the influential human rights group, the Citizen's Constitutional Forum. He pulled no punches. Speight was 'a two-day wonder' with 'no real track record of fighting for indigenous rights'. He championed indigenous rights 'for his own personal reasons'. When asked to name the coup's backers, he referred to parliamentarians who had not criticised the coup.

And there are others like Duvuloco just turned out from the woodwork and wants to be a minister now. He had fought elections five times and lost five times. Why should he become a minister? . . . They just mobilise poor Fijians who really don't understand what they are doing. They are genuine but they don't know the agenda of these people who have actually manipulated them to support the coup.[72]

Dakuvula's words were like a red flag to a bull. Within an hour, a mob of 100 men – led by armed rebels – left the parliamentary complex and headed for Fiji TV's offices. On the way they fired four shots at the President's palace, smashed the TV station, putting it off air, threatened staff at Radio Fiji, and fired shots into the Centra Hotel, where most foreign journalists were staying. During the rampage one policeman was shot and a security guard died of heart failure.

These were not the only threats journalists received. Two days later, rebels threatened FM96 reporters. Its newsreader was told that if 'we kept calling them terrorists, rebels or bandits the same thing . . . that happened to Fiji TV would happen to us'.[73] Some preachers were no better. The *Fiji Sun* quoted one church minister telling his congregation that God removed Chaudhry because unbelievers could never rule Fiji. The Church minister retaliated. 'I know each and everyone of you from your reporters to your boss,' he threatened. 'I will come in and shoot each of you and burn the place down.'[74]

Suva's descent into mob rule deliberately raised the ante. Around Fiji the same thing occurred, particularly in isolated Indian communities where whole families were being terrorised or their homes looted and razed.

But in Suva the initial target had been Mara, the violence simply a measure of rebel frustration at his elusiveness. Mara was vulnerable. His daughter, Adi Koila Nailatikau Mara, was one of the MPs still held hostage by the rebels. They had already threatened her life.[75] Indeed, they let it be known that they intended to march on Government House, the presidential palace. Alarmed, the President's private secretary, Jo Browne, sent an officer early on Sunday morning to collect ammunition for the platoon guarding the President. At 8.00 a.m. Bainimarama, Rabuka and Savua arrived to brief Mara on the security situation but suddenly left without meeting the President. Later Browne became aware that their guards had disappeared.[76]

Browne and Mara were perplexed, but unbeknown to them the same puzzling tactic was being employed at Veiuto. Troops were withdrawn. The police warned people to stay at home. 'Each time a bluff is not called,' the *Australian*'s foreign editor Greg Sheridan wrote, 'the price of ultimately calling it increases hugely.' As Fiji's crisis lurched into a new phase, the CRWU's bluff had now become the power.[77]

Mara contacted his son at the military barracks and was assured of protection. It never arrived. Instead, that evening, without notice, Mara and his family were hastily evacuated to a naval vessel in Suva Harbour. 'I didn't have time to … even ask a question,' Mara complained.[78]

While the rebels released their frustration on Suva, Mara waited patiently. One night passed. By Monday afternoon (29 May) the army had reimposed barricades around the parliamentary area. Commentators believed that a showdown loomed. But Bainimarama had other plans. That evening he visited Mara with a military delegation that also included Rabuka and Savua. He wanted to end the stand-off with the rebels once and for all. 'All the nation has been saddened by the extent to which the country has fallen during the last week,' Bainimarama told the nation a few hours later. Worse, Savua now believed that his police could no longer guarantee the security of the state.[79] They were both of the opinion that the Constitution provided no 'framework for resolving the crisis', and that to persist with it 'threatened the peace, order and internal security of the Republic'.[80] Accordingly, the delegation asked Mara to stand aside for 21 days. 'They want me out; they want to abrogate the Constitution and this is exactly what Speight wants,' Mara thought as he received their presentation. He 'felt betrayed by the custodians of security who served under him. Yes', he told them. 'To avoid bloodshed, yes. But he would never come back'.[81] The next day the navy took him to his home village on Lakeba in the eastern Lau islands.

CONFRONTING THE MILITARY

Mara's sudden departure signalled a new and totally unexpected intervention by the military. Now 'no elected government', the *Fiji Times* later editorialised, 'could ever feel safe'.[82] All the CRWU demands had now been met. Chaudhry's Government had been dismissed, Mara had gone, and the Constitution jettisoned. But Speight wanted much more. He wanted the

Bau chief Ratu Jope Seniloli to replace Mara as President and his own Taukei Civilian Government appointed, with himself as Prime Minister. 'I'm telling the military to back off,' he retorted. 'The military came in at the twelfth hour. They have effectively performed a coup and I find that quite ironic.'[83]

If the military's push against Speight raised popular hopes for a quick resolution to the crisis, they were soon dashed. The 48-hour curfew Bainimarama imposed on assuming office as Head of State was lifted within a day. Despite the barricades and containers placed around Parliament, ostensibly to ensure that only essential goods entered, hundreds of coup supporters continued to stream into the complex. The rebels also continued to commit acts of violence with impunity. Passing cars were stoned and on Tuesday 10 taxis were hijacked and driven to the Parliament. Several rebels were arrested for breaking the curfew and beaten; they were all released. Reports from the compound suggested that such acts of wanton violence only incensed the crowds further. And Ligairi was said to have lost control of his supporters.

In reality Ligairi had organised his supporters into units, each representing provincial groupings. He trained them and made them march very publicly around the compound. But they were also used around Suva to create disturbances and keep the city on edge. On Wednesday a mob of 50 youths attacked police, injuring three. Further confrontations continued during the week.

Parliamentary communication systems were also put to good use. Newsletters, faxes, and phone calls flowed from the offices and across the country, creating rumours, fomenting disorder, and wooing support. In downtown Suva, shopkeepers took no chances; they placed containers in front of their shops.

Even the military's political proposals brought no certainty. It signalled that in six months time it would appoint an interim civilian government to put in place a new Constitution and hold elections within three years, an objective not too different from Mara's. It even proposed former army commander Ratu Epeli Nailatikau (husband of hostage Adi Koila) as Prime Minister. But unlike Mara, it agreed to award places in this interim government to the rebels. By this means the army hoped to resolve the hostage situation.

Speight rejected its proposal. The military 'poses no threat to me', he scoffed. 'It won't rise up against its own people.'[84] Buoyant again, Speight now wanted nothing less than his own Taukei Civilian Government firmly in place. Seeking a way out of the impasse, Bainimarama told his officers that he intended to negotiate with Speight to get the hostages released and 'let the army complete the takeover'. A large military delegation travelled to the parliamentary complex to signal their commander's intention.[85] On Thursday evening Bainimarama met Speight for the first time and agreed to a remarkable compromise. The Great Council of Chiefs would decide the country's future: a military government or a civilian administration that might well be Speight's Taukei Civilian Government.

That evening military spokesperson, Lieutenant Colonel Filipo Tarakinikini, tried to justify the military capitulation. Tellingly, he employed the rebel's propaganda uncritically.

Their breaking of the law stemmed from their dissatisfaction with the government of the day and the Constitution, also regulations that they saw were being passed. 'They told us 42 acts had gone through Parliament and passed into law. I'm not sure how accurate that is, but within the process of 12 months! . . . They say that all these are designed to weaken the rights and the security of Fijians, indigenous Fijians, in their own land. So that's the thing that led to the uprising. We cannot ignore the political side of it . . . it is not purely criminal.'[86]

The implications of 'we accept your cause but not your methods' now drove the military inexorably towards accommodation.

Nonetheless, when Bainimarama briefed officers the next morning, they were alarmed. The proposed compromise carried too many risks. They were not prepared to place the country's future in the hands of an institution already tainted by close links with Speight. They argued that many chiefs connived with the rebels for their own selfish ends and Speight was no more than an opportunist. To compromise now risked more bloodshed in the future.

But they did not propose restoring the Constitution. It was dead, and with it the former Coalition Government still held hostage in Parliament.

Only three political players remained — the rebels, the chiefs, and the military — and these younger officers had no intention of surrendering the military's role as guardian of the nation. Instead they proposed a public campaign to win back the support of dissident Fijians. That evening the thirty-nine-year-old Tarakinikini began the campaign with a national radio address.

> What is now happening to us is a moral recession in the sense [that] the very values, the very core of our existence, is being challenged . . . Speight and his group are a formidable lot. They know what they are doing, and they are applying tactics that have succeeded elsewhere in the world. They will threaten and they will try and destabilise and fragment our community so we will become vulnerable, and we will play into their hands if we succumb to tactics of fear.

Speight, he said, claimed that all Fijian problems could be resolved with a Constitution guaranteeing absolute Fijian paramountcy. This is too simplistic. 'The only way we indigenous Fijians will succeed is to make sure we make sacrifices today for the sake of our prosperity tomorrow,'. 'This is the time for us to stand up and defend the democracy we believe in, where each man is created equal in the eyes of God,' a democracy that stresses good governance, accountability and transparency.[87]

The stalemate produced further uncertainty. Some western chiefs declared that they would not attend any future meeting of the Great Council of Chiefs called to decide between the rebels and the military. Each time a government had been led by a western Prime Minister and enjoyed better western representation in Cabinet, it had been overthrown. They talked now of forming a separate government. But they were far from united and eventually, after much discussion, they called for an early return to civilian government and declared that Fiji should be a Christian state.

Chiefs from Naitasiri and Tailevu provinces were also far from united, although rumours suggested that close personal relations between members of the Speight family and the Cakobau dynasty now generated a new political dynamic for the rebels to exploit. The general manager of the Native

Land Trust Board, Maika Qarikau, provided another. His organisation had begun circulating a 'Deed of Sovereignty', modelled on the 1874 Deed of Cession which had, nationalists alleged, 'entrusted' Fijian sovereignty to colonial authorities. Qarikau's Deed now urged chiefs to entrust their sovereignty to the Civilian Taukei Government. Chiefs 'were supposed to be the voice of reason, the voice of wisdom', Chief Justice Sir Timoci Tuivaga reflected sadly. 'But they are at war among themselves.'[88] So too, it seemed, were his colleagues, especially after Tuivaga and two other judges helped draft the military decree which abrogated the Constitution. 'Good intentions,' the Law Society's president argued, 'cannot take precedence over a judge's solemn duty to uphold the Constitution.'[89]

Speight, meanwhile, continued to employ his 'dogs of war' to tease the military. Early on Wednesday 7 June (Day 20 of the crisis) sporadic shooting broke out near the Parliament and continued for one hour. The next day rebel supporters attacked a policeman sent to retrieve stolen vehicles in the parliamentary compound. Speight shrugged it off as 'just one of those things'.[90] Three days later his 'dogs of war' attacked a checkpoint and wounded two soldiers. They also burnt down a nearby restaurant on the beachfront. On Monday 12 June frustrated soldiers shot at Speight's car as it sped through a military roadblock. An angry Speight claimed divine intervention saved him from assassination.

That night former FIS boss, Metuisela Mua, went on Australian television to warn the military that the rebels had plans to target military and other installations across the country if the army did not cave in. 'Thereafter the problem will be a recurring problem,' he threatened. 'It will never heal.'[91] The next day Tarakinikini admitted that the army had become disillusioned at its inability to end the crisis after two weeks. Already Indian refugees were flooding westward from isolated settlements in Tailevu and Naitasiri seeking sanctuary from marauding gangs of Fijians. The military take over provided no relief for them; nor for people living in the suburbs near the parliamentary complex, who were subjected to daily raids from rebel supporters. Earlier Bainimarama had announced that the military's civilian administration would soon be formed and that the constitution would be rewritten to restore democracy to all communities. Now Tarakinikini admitted that if the chiefs decided to support Speight, the military would be in an untenable situation. 'What's going on now is a revolution. It is a revolution in Fijian society and it will last a long time.'

A revolution, moreover, which also threatened to engulf the military. Already 36 of its soldiers were among the rebels. Now many CRWU soldiers who had remained at the military barracks were also missing. They were not at the Parliament. No one knew where they were.[92]

On Thursday 15 June (Day 28) the chiefs did intervene. Ratu Josefa Iloilo, the western-based Tui Vuda and Mara's former Vice President, offered his services as a mediator, and talks between the rebels and the military began at his residence in Muanikau (a suburb neighbouring Veiuto). While Fiji awaited the outcome, many chiefs began to pledge support for the military, in part the consequence of lobbying by nine military public relations teams touring Fiji's provinces. But the chiefs left their options open, demanding also that the Great Council of Chiefs meet again soon. Some chiefs disagreed. Speight only turned to the GCC because he believed he could get a better deal from them, they argued. Fiji could disintegrate into tribal warfare if its chiefs allowed themselves to be used.[93]

Meanwhile the talks dragged on, in part because the rebel team kept changing its negotiators. The army wearied. It agreed to the Great Council of Chiefs meeting to elect a President and Vice President. It agreed also to hand power to a civilian administration appointed by the President, subject to the release of the hostages. The rebels 'have got the upper hand now; they're almost dictating the terms of the negotiations and the military have been back-peddling', Rabuka claimed. 'So much has been given to [Speight]; . . . If he plays his cards right he could be President.'[94]

But at 11.00 a.m. on the day of the official signing of the Muanikau Accord, Saturday 24 June (Day 37), Speight over-played his hand. Ligairi refused to release the hostages until all their demands were met.

When George went out (to negotiate) I told him clearly – remember our demand is to have some of our people in government; so that when we go from here, our people are sitting here. If we don't do that, the hostages won't be released.[95]

Consequently Speight arrived at Iloilo's residence with a new set of demands designed to reduce the likelihood of any negative outcome from the Chiefs' meeting. Ratu Iloilo must be President and Ratu Jope Seniloli Vice President. And the army must hand over power within a week. Ten minutes later Bainimarama walked out in frustration. 'You can't walk straight along a crooked path,' Tarakinikini quipped.

To demonstrate good faith, the rebels released the four female hostages, but continued to push their claims aggressively. They declared that even with an accord, they would not lay down their arms. They needed weapons for their future protection. In the parliamentary grounds, groups of young Fijians were paraded provocatively. Tarakinikini confessed that his troops were itching to get at the 'toy soldiers'.

I thought it was a simple thing of political agendas, but they got into this mode of sowing the seeds of revolution and poisoning the minds of our people, who are really gullible and vulnerable to these kinds of tactics.

Tarakinikini blamed Ligairi.

You can see the tactics – discrediting, trying to destabilise, training boys from villages in how to handle weapons. That's how you raise an ... insurrection in a country where communism has set in. That's the thing that disappoints me most. [Ligairi] has been trained by the Brits and he has come home to retire and he now thinks he is going to sow the seeds of revolution in our own country. I will not accept that ...[96]

But short of invading Parliament, which the army had always ruled out because of the hostages, Tarakinikini could do little.

On Tuesday 27 June the military gave the rebels 24 hours to sign the accord. They refused. 'They're just playing at it day by day; they don't know when to stop,' Rabuka argued. The coup had become a farce and its supporters were nothing but 'losers',[97] he added. But some commentators assigned responsibility more widely. 'The paucity of leadership in the country is staggering,' reported *Australian* journalist Christopher Dore. Mara had vanished, Rabuka sulked in his office, and Bainimarama had not spoken publicly for two weeks. His military council had 'never emerged from the shadows'. The Great Council of Chiefs had also disappeared, its liaison committee mired in conspiracies with the rebels. And in the Parliament the scheming continued, its leaders bickering over 'whose coup it really is'. 'No-one in Fiji', said Dore, 'has the slightest clue about how to end the political crisis'.[98]

Once more a showdown loomed. On Thursday 29 June (Day 42) the military threatened an exclusion zone around Parliament. Speight responded that he could not guarantee the safety of his hostages if the army attacked. An uneasy stalemate set in, broken only on the following Tuesday when the military finally announced the formation of an interim government led by the wealthy former Fiji Development Bank head and senator, 59-year-old Lauan Laisenia Qarase. With him came an 18-strong all-male Cabinet charged with guiding Fiji to elections within two years. In his acceptance speech, Qarase promised to introduce a new Constitution, to improve services to Fijians, and to amend land leases along the lines favoured by the NLTB. The Fijian bureaucratic establishment was once more in charge. The army had injected a more conservative alternative for the chiefs to consider. In time it would once again become a major player in its own right.

None of these Cabinet members 'ever fought for the cause of the take over', Ligairi responded. They had failed Fiji in the past and would do so again.[99] Speight was livid: 'We didn't carry out the coup to provide an opportunity for the military to come in and run the government – that's not the objective of the coup and they don't seem to accept that.'[100] These initiatives would have repercussions, he warned. Indeed they did, and more quickly than anyone imagined.

At 1.00 p.m. in Labasa, capital of Vanua Levu, the second largest island, 80 soldiers under the command of Ligairi's grandson, Lieutenant Rupeni Vosayaco, and assisted by former politician Ratu Josefa Dimuri and some

500 supporters, seized control of the Sukanaivalu Barracks and its armoury at Vaturekuka. Immediately the city shut down. Two hours later in Suva 200 rebels and soldiers clashed outside the Parliament. Five rebels were wounded (one of whom died five days later) and 14 arrested. The next day, as the military announced the imposition of its exclusion zone, Speight issued another warning. Soon chiefs will resist the army and call on Fijians to leave it, he declared. 'As that takes place over the next few days, I'm sure Commander Bainimarama will find himself in command of an army that has no men.'[101]

As if on cue, crowds of Naitasiri villagers gathered on Thursday at Suva's Vunidawa, Laqere and Kalabu suburbs to march on the army headquarters in Nabua to protest the army's exclusion zone. Rumours suggested an uprising had started. At the same time a young medical assistant, fresh from Suva's parliamentary battlefields, presented kava to soldiers guarding Monasavu's power facilities in Naitisiri's highlands. It was drugged. Rebel sympathisers quickly disrupted power supply and plunged Suva into further crisis.[102]

While chiefs of Macuata Province in the north demanded Bainimarama step down, the paramount chief of Naitisiri Province – the Turaga na Qaranivalu Ratu Inoke Takiveikata – led a delegation to the Nabua barracks to petition for a civilian President elected by the Great Council of Chiefs. Hundreds of villagers waited outside while he met with senior officers. A second petition demanded compensation for all their land currently occupied by the Crown, including semi-urban land around Suva containing schools and the FMF headquarters. 'Their grievance is really quite touching,' Tarakinikini conceded.[103]

Overwhelmed by this apparently well-orchestrated campaign of civil disobedience, the military leaders met and decided to cave in to demands that the Great Council of Chiefs meet and elect a President who would then choose his own interim administration. 'We don't want to shed blood among ourselves,' Tarakinikini declared. Pragmatism ruled.[104]

On Friday the army met with the rebels. It reported its meeting as the outcome of chiefly intervention or mediation by Takiveikata. The rebels would 'surrender' in two days time. In return for laying down their weapons and releasing their hostages by Thursday next week, they would receive immunity from prosecution.

On Sunday evening 9 July (Day 52) the Muanikau Accord was finally signed at Iloilo's residence, watched by some 500 hymn-chanting rebel supporters. Bainimarama kept his head bowed during the solemn ceremony and avoided eye contact with the rebel leader. The exuberant Speight, as always resplendent in his clothes, presented a remarkable contrast to the people around him. Christopher Dore reported:

> A foreign journalist offers a running commentary just a little too loudly, providing an absurd soundtrack to an already bizarre event, making it all the more delicious for Speight. 'Army Commander Frank Bainimarama looks decidedly unhappy,' the journalist inadvertently bellows down the line. Speight smiles, the army cringes, the nation sits stunned and horrified.[105]

Tarakinikini tried to play down the significance of the accord.

> [To] fully address the cause and aspirations of the indigenous Fijians, that is a long, long journey, and if someone is claiming that victory has already been won for the cause of indigenous Fijians by the signing of the Muanikau Accord, then I think that their views on Fijian aspirations were very super-ficial to start with.[106]

Speight was in no mood to quibble. Having worn down the military and struck an accord more to his liking, he now fixed his mind on the chiefs.

CONFRONTING THE CHIEFS

The rebel accord with the military did not end civil disobedience. Instead it escalated. Roadblocks sprang up around Suva and elsewhere in Fiji. One hundred and fifty rebels led by one CRWU soldier seized Korovou, a rural town in Tailevu Province, and detained some 30 policemen. This set a new standard for protest despite the Muanikau Accord, or rather because of it. The rebels had silenced the army; they had now to remind the chiefs that Fiji's future was really in rebel hands.

In Vanua Levu, villagers seized the Savusavu and Seaqaqa police stations. Central Labasa itself came under siege. In addition Fijians threatened Telecom facilities in Labasa, Nadi airport, the army base at Lautoka, even Suva's Central Police Station. On Ovalau island, villagers attacked the Levuka police station and, on the basis of rumours alleging a Masonic conspiracy and secret tunnels, destroyed the town's old Masonic Lodge. They also occupied the local fish cannery, the town's main employer.

Over the next week Fijian groups seized many police posts around the country, although often for reasons only vaguely connected with the coup. Land grievances or alleged discriminatory employment policies formed the basis for many of the actions. In the Yasawa group of islands, landowners seized the Turtle Island resort. Landowners also seized the Laucala Island resort and a new mineral water plant in Rakiraki. Other occupations occurred at the Buca Bay resort and Rukuruku Resort. On Vanuabalavu, landowners closed the airstrip, demanding job preferences. Fijian Telecom workers went on strike. Landowners and disgruntled employees occupied Road Transport Department offices in Suva and Lautoka. Prisoners at Naboro Prison outside of Suva rioted and took 26 wardens hostage, before staging a mass breakout.

Rebel Jo Nata bragged: 'Suva is almost under siege; the whole nation is in chaos. We are in control of the northern part and most parts of Viti Levu – is that what you call holding a gun to the chief's heads?' Only when the chiefs 'put the right people in place' will the rebels declare it 'time to call off the dogs', he declared.[107]

And Speight had another tactic for influencing the chiefs. Earlier in the week the deputy chair of the Great Council of Chiefs, Adi Litia Cakobau, called a special council of district and provincial chiefs (*Bose ni Turaga*) to meet one day before the Great Council of Chiefs[108]. Adi Litia's sister, Adi Samanunu Cakobau, flew from Malaysia (where she was Fiji's ambassador) to chair the meeting. But some of the 200 chiefs attending the meeting were horrified at what they observed. 'They have stopped listening to their chiefs', the chair of the Ra Provincial Council exclaimed when his own high chief was detained at Korovou by rebels. 'So we ask, what comes next?'[109]

By the time the meeting concluded, it had determined that Iloilo should be President, Seniloli his deputy, and Samanunu's uncle, Ratu Epeli Kanaimawi, Prime Minister. Kanaimawi would head a 22-member Cabinet with at least 11 rebel supporters. In addition, the *Bose ni Turaga* recommended a 14-member Constitutional Review Committee headed by Professor Asesela Ravuvu. The next day the long-awaited Great Council of Chiefs began its deliberations.

By Friday 14 July (Day 57) Speight had achieved some of his objectives. The chiefs did appoint Iloilo, but as Vice President he had been next in succession in any case. The appointment of rebel Seniloli as Vice President was much more significant, not only because the position enabled him to influence Iloilo's selection of Prime Minister, but also because Iloilo was 80 years old, a victim of Parkinson's disease, and ailing. Seniloli could reasonably assume to succeed Iloilo in the near future. Nonetheless, Speight warned that while it was up to Iloilo to decide the make-up of the new government, 'the people of Fiji, the people I have represented, have made it very clear what sort of government they want'.[110]

Satisfied, the rebels released their 18 remaining hostages and proudly showed off to journalists their cache of weapons ('dozens of automatic weapons including Uzis, a collection of handguns, a few grenade launchers, some Claymore mines, and enough ammo to fight a small war')[111] before surrendering them to the military. But despite emerging as winners, Fiji's new Tontons Macoutes had yet to learn the final outcome of the chiefs' meeting.

THE MILITARY STRIKES BACK

Qarase addressed the chiefs on the second day of their meeting and presented a well-prepared blueprint to enhance Fijian rights. As we shall see later, none of the strategies proposed were original. Indeed they had been tried before. But if nothing else Qarase was organised and professional, and his proposals clearly addressed the special interests of Fiji's bureaucratic and chiefly elites. He even presented a timetable for developing a new Constitution ahead of fresh elections in two years time.

The chiefs were impressed. In any case, no-one else presented an alternative plan. Speight's group focused solely on personnel and threats, not strategies. 'As we have said before, there are people acting independently in support of us,' Nata warned, as the rebels buried in the Parliament grounds their comrade cut down in the recent skirmish with the army. 'We will not be able to control them if the new government consists of people who are not acceptable to our supporters.'[112] The threat had bite. The military announced many rebel weapons were missing.

That afternoon Iloilo announced that Qarase's administration would remain. Only a few changes had been made to accommodate Speight supporters. Significantly, two Coalition ministers were in the 32-person (there were now four women) line-up and one Opposition Indian. Speight reacted bitterly: 'It's totally unacceptable to us. It will result in a serious backlash,' he variously told journalists. 'I think some people are trying to do me over and they're going to meet with some very stiff resistance . . . The fun is just beginning. These people are blind.'[113]

At 11.00 a.m. on Wednesday 19 July (Day 62) Qarase's Cabinet waited to be sworn in. Iloilo did not appear. Officially he was ill. Speight had made many phone calls the night before, but Adi Samanunu's visit to the President in the morning proved more effective. At the time Speight did not know this. He and his rebels were preparing to leave the parliamentary complex to base themselves at Kalabu, 12km from Suva Central, where some 500 supporters were already gathered for a welcoming feast. Speight vented his anger against Qarase and his line-up: 'While I was being called a rebel, a terrorist and a thug, they hid, protecting their reputations and names. It is by my sweat that they are now being considered for the interim government.'[114] His dogs of war again embarked on another round of destruction and looting.[115]

Once established at Kalabu, the rebels again pressured Iloilo. Savua convened a meeting at the Central Police Station with Takiveikata, Ligairi and the new Vice President's secretary to 'start the ball rolling' on a new set of rebel demands,[116] including that the 60-year-old Adi Samanunu replace Qarase as Prime Minister. Samanunu's elevation further signalled the increasing role of the Cakobau family in the rebel intrigues. A rebel spokesperson claimed that she 'was a symbol of stability and guidance for the people and the chiefs during the crisis'.[117] Yet her support for the rebels also represented another chapter in the Cakobau family's long struggle to restore itself to national prominence and to eclipse the rival Mara family. In the nineteenth century the Cakobaus held sway over much of Fiji; during the twentieth century chiefs from Lau rose to prominence. This struggle introduced yet another dynamic in the already fractious relationships between Fijian provinces and between old centres of power.

In response to rebel demands, the President informed the nation he would probably include more rebel supporters in the Cabinet, but he was slower in delivering on this than the rebels liked. For its part, the army now publicly condemned the pressure applied to Iloilo by the rebels, and retaliated with increased roadblocks around Kalabu. Foreign Affairs questioned why Adi Samanunu had left her diplomatic post without permission. Home Affairs told Savua to stop participating in the talks.[118] On 26 July the rebel negotiating team met with Iloilo. Speight was blunt. If Iloilo did not 'change his mind about the line-up of the interim government there would be further instability in the country'.[119] This was no idle threat; a background of latent insecurity kept the nation on edge.[120] Iloilo caved in. The news quickly reached Bainimarama. He rushed to the President's office.

He rejected Mr Speight's demands. He could not stand by and watch traitors appointed to high office. He issued an ultimatum of his own: 'Get a Prime Minister of our choice, or else lose the army.' Ratu Iloilo conceded, agreeing to confirm Mr Qarase in the role. Leaving the presidential villa with this undertaking, Commodore Bainimarama then moved swiftly and ruthlessly to head off further manoeuvring by the rebels.[121]

That evening at 11.00 p.m. George Speight, his bodyguard, lawyer Tevita Bukarau, and Jo Nata were arrested not far from Kalabu as they returned to their camp, and were later imprisoned in isolation on Nukulau island in Suva Harbour. Their disappearance alerted no one at the Kalabu rebel camp. Shortly after 6.00 a.m. the next morning, the military struck, taking the sleeping rebels by surprise. The result: 369 rebels arrested (including 12 CRWU soldiers), one rebel dead, and 33 rebels hospitalised.

Hostile responses to the military crackdown were sporadic and confined mainly to Vanua Levu. Rebel sympathisers razed Mara's Seaqaqa cane farm and seized the Labasa police station. Several Labasa Indians were rounded up and taken to the Sukanivalu Barracks, sparking fears of a new hostage crisis. In Savusavu two New Zealand Air Fiji pilots were seized. Eventually the military regained control.[122] But the malaise within the Fijian community continued. Wounded and divided, there now existed a heightened sense of distrust, fear and loathing.

FIJIAN DISUNITY: FEAR, LOATHING AND MUTINY

For a short while, Fiji enjoyed a kind of calm, nervously relieved that the hostage crisis was at long last over and the menace of violence gone. The Monasavu rebels released their 30 military hostages at the end of July, transformed themselves back into long-aggrieved compensation claimants for the land electric power generation occupied, and won a settlement worth $52 million. At the start of August the army stormed the Labasa barracks and, with the loss of only one rebel life, secured 70 prisoners. Military decisiveness had returned.

Over the rest of that month some 120 rebels were arrested in a sweep across Vanua Levu and charges of treason laid against Speight, Ligairi and 15 co-conspirators. The High Court declared the Muanikau amnesty invalid and investigations began into the activities of more than 250 people within and outside the military. Savua was forced to step aside as police commissioner to allow the Chief Justice, himself under public scrutiny for assisting the military to seize power on 29 May, to conduct an investigation into his activities during the crisis.

But the calm was uneasy and the army had to cope with new forms of harassment, including of soldiers. Tarakinikini proved too articulate and ambitious for many of his superiors, and lost his post as army spokesperson in September. Disillusioned, in March 2001 he took up a peacekeeping post with the United Nations in New York[123]. Bainimarama also became a target, particularly of chiefly anger, after he admonished them for instigating division and hate among Fijians. 'There is one set of rules for everyone', he warned, 'and we must all understand that.'[124] But many chiefs refused to. It was the army that caused all Fiji's crises, one western chief retorted. 'Maybe his leadership is a problem', another chief asserted. 'They should do the right thing and sort that problem out first.'[125]

Bainimarama was not the only Fijian leader under the spotlight. When President Iloilo prepared for medical tests in Sydney, the army refused to accept the rebel nominated Vice President Seniloli as his replacement. Radio Fiji reported the military's threat to take over if Seniloli acted as President. In the uproar that followed, Rabuka raised his hand and offered to serve as President. The target of loathing shifted again.

This climate of distrust presented dangers. 'The further up the investigations went, the tighter the noose around the necks of the powerful backers of Speight and his gang, the greater the likelihood the rebels would rise again,' observed journalist Tony Parkinson.[126] In addition many of the rebels caught were beaten and resented the treatment they received from the military. Most of them had been charged only with minor offences, and were quickly released on very lenient bail terms by the Chief Magistrate.

At the Nabua army headquarters the 12 detained CRWU soldiers smarted at their treatment. They were convinced that the army planned to disband their unit. 'We felt betrayed by Bainimarama', rebel soldier Serupepeli Dakai declared.

'When the Muanikau Accord was signed, we gave up our weapons in good faith. We had nothing to do with the weapons that went missing and we thought he should honour the agreement . . . Instead look at what they did to those in Parliament. We were not happy with the way the military threatened the civilians, especially those at Kalabu.'[127]

The elite unit felt ostracised, 'left out in the cold', 'strangers in the camp'.[128] Even the apparently loyal Captain Shane Stevens turned. The military, of course, had been taunted and fired at by CRWU rebels and deeply resented its inability to strike back because of the human shields the CRWU employed. These tensions in the camp remained unresolved.

Although the rebels faced possible court martial and some 150 soldiers were said to be under investigation, the army treated its rebels leniently. In early October the Director of Public Prosecutions withdrew charges of treason against eight of their number on the grounds that they only followed orders. In the same week that both Iloilo and Qarase were out of the country, Bainimarama released the detained CRWU soldiers in the spirit of reconciliation. 'I told them we will let the law take its course, but in the meantime they could go home and enjoy life with their families.' Howard Politini, now the army's main public relations officer, even praised them. 'The people should realise that these soldiers were responsible for the security of the hostages in Parliament and they did a good job,' he said. 'They were well trained and had the power to contain the rowdy and abusive crowd.'[129] Three days later, on Thursday 2 November, the CRWU mutinied.

It was a bloody and confused affair. Forty soldiers headed by Stevens seized weapons and took over Bainimarama's office, the national operations centre and the armoury. They wanted hostages; above all they wanted Bainimarama. Yet they executed three unarmed loyal soldiers in cold blood. Again their planning was meagre; the whole operation designed simply as a repeat of May 19. Several minutes before 1.00 p.m., an unsigned fax ordered Vodaphone to shut down many army mobiles. A coded message over Radio Fiji told Naitisiri, Tailevu and Rewa provincial organisers to get as many human shields into the camp as possible. The rebels planned to negotiate for the release of all their colleagues on Nukulau, re-establish the Taukei Civilian Government, and replace Bainimarama. Instead the operation collapsed.

For a start the rebels were unable to secure ammunition for the weapons they seized and had to make do with a more limited range of standard-issue weapons. Second, they botched the attack on Bainimarama and the senior command. Instead of employing stealth, they 'brazenly assembled at the camp ground, conspicuous in their black T-shirts' and fired 'warning shots as they dispersed towards their targets'.[130] Third, they gave little thought to how the wider army might be neutralised. In fact, elements of the Third Fiji Infantry Regiment returned from field exercises in Nadroga Province just as the mutiny erupted and quickly mounted a counter offensive. Fourth, loyal troops discovered the plot to bus in human shields and closed the camp gates.

By the end of the day, the battle for Nabua was over. Eight soldiers lay dead, five of them rebels allegedly beaten to death after their arrest. At least one dead CRWU soldier had not participated in the mutiny. He had been arrested and brought to the camp after the event. In addition, 20 soldiers were injured and stray bullets hit six civilians.[131]

But military victory over the mutineers brought no peace. Instead it intensified recriminations. Rabuka became one of the early victims. Since 1997 Rabuka had been feted internationally for bringing Fiji back from the abyss he had driven it to. He had been honoured internationally with the Solomon Islands dispute to resolve. But the year 2000 had not been kind to Rabuka. Each time 'the Statesman' inserted himself into the dramas around him, he created suspicion, not respect. Mara accused him of conspiracy; Speight and Ligairi of betrayal. Now Bainimarama accused him of treachery. He came to the barracks uninvited just as the military counter attack began. He threatened to put on his uniform and return as commander if the assault team was not withdrawn. He criticised the commander's leadership. He left with one of the rebels in his car. Bainimarama suspected Rabuka was trying to buy time until the human shields arrived. 'He really confuses the army, that man,' Bainimarama declared.[132]

Rabuka told it differently. Having flown in from Savusavu, he was lunching when his personal assistant informed him of the mutiny. He first called Colonel Seruvakula of the Third Fiji Infantry Regiment, and then Home

Affairs, before speaking to a number of people at the camp. One of the rebels asked him to mediate because he disapproved of the mutiny; the same man later left with Rabuka. Rabuka also spoke with one of the hostages. At this point he decided that he was needed. But he got there too late. The orders to attack had been issued.[133]

Rabuka denied any part in the mutiny. He did not approve of the rebels' goals. 'We should allow ourselves to evolve into a vibrant society of mixed races, [a] multiethnic, multiracial, multireligious society,' he declared. 'Those who are trying to drag us back into the era of the dinosaur . . . hopefully will quickly be called to their graves.' Meanwhile he would continue to work for a new Fiji: 'I cannot let the flame that inspired me to work towards the 1997 Constitution . . . burn out.'[134] But the knives were out for Rabuka. In March 2001 the Great Council of Chiefs dumped him as their chairman. Bainimarama also came under scrutiny. He believed that everything he had done during the course of 2000 had been designed to foster stability and reconciliation among indigenous Fijians. He usurped authority on 29 May to protect the President and save Fiji from descending into anarchy. He refused to raid Parliament for fear that the deaths of inno-cent or naive Fijians would produce an even greater backlash against the army. He backed Qarase's regime because it alone promised Fijians a clearly articulated direction.

But these goals did not accord with international conventions, let alone satisfy Fiji's other communities. They felt excluded. So, too, many business people. The Qarase regime's plans for a new Constitution threatened to bring international retaliation and the loss of important markets for Fiji's products. Its chaotic approach to land use threatened Fiji's agricultural production and a new wave of rural refugees. But for many people, including Fijians, it was the sense of déjà vu that was most disillusioning. Thirteen years of patience and consensus building had come to nought.

The reassertion of Fijian paramountcy posed many threats, not least of all to Fijians themselves. 'If Indians are forced to leave Fiji', Mara told his Lau Provincial Council, 'the next group of people will be islanders who have made a living in Viti Levu.'[135] Indeed, the more Fiji moved towards

the kind of traditional *vanua* (Fijian community) politics, he now recommended, the more fractious the *vanua* became. Exclusive notions of identity
have a habit of becoming more exclusive and targets of envy shift. Rabuka
noted how even moderate provincial successes created envy in other provinces,
and encouraged self-pity.[136] What Fijians really needed was to come to terms
with their own history and their own modernity. The past offered no justice
or direction to the thousands of Fijians who had abandoned the poverty of
their villages for the poverty of urban slums. And they had also to come
to terms with the reality of Fiji's multiculturalism. The past offered no
guide for the future.

Nor did Qarase's Government. Its Blueprint for Fijian Development
advantaged the Fijian middle classes, not the disaffected masses that had
fuelled the CRWU rebellion. Education, which Bainimarama believed essential for Fijian development, received no boost in the first Qarase budget.
In fact, government grants to secondary schools halved and, although
special funding was set aside for Fijian education, not a cent reached them
if they went to multi-ethnic schools, as so many Fijians did in the cities.[137]

Although aware of these divisions, neither Bainimarama nor Qarase could
suggest anything other than reconciliation to resolve the indigenous question. But how? Bainimarama conceded that the only thing that united Fijians
was their opposition to Indians, but it was hardly a strategy for reconciliation. It had already created too much strife and misery.[138]

Qarase created a Ministry of Reconciliation and launched a National
Council Reconciliation and Unity in late November. It proposed the educational integration of Fiji's communities, racial parity in the military, and
a new national identity. It also planned a special program in 2002 to
prepare young chiefs for leadership.[139] But for the present it could only
plead that Fiji's peoples be more forgiving of each other. 'One needed to
forgive unconditionally before attempting reconciliation', Qarase told the
National Tourism Forum in December, 'because unity was impossible without
forgiveness.'[140]

Forgiveness included Speight. 'There are so many people with much
worse records who got away free right around the world,' he declared.[141]

Rabuka agreed. He told the Cakaudrove Provincial Council that the courts should consider reconciliation as part of the endeavour to unite the people of Fiji and give sentences accordingly.[142] Qarase's Permanent Secretary for Reconciliation even declared investigations at the Nabua barracks an obstacle to reconciliation.[143] The dropping of charges 'for lack of evidence' against four rebel leaders held on Nukulau – including Mua and Bukarau – encouraged this line of action. 'If Fiji is to go forward,' one of the freed rebels declared, 'the reconciliation process must start on Nukulau.' And in the public service, too. On the Chief Justice's recommendation, Savua was reinstated as Police Commissioner in November. In May the following year a public service inquiry also cleared Adi Samanunu of any wrong-doing.

There were dangers in this approach. A disgusted Seruvakula left the command of the Third Fiji Infantry in March 2001 and, with three other officers, began service with the New Zealand Defence Forces. Already New Zealand's High Commissioner, Tia Barrett, had very publicly condemned Fiji's apparent reluctance to bring to justice 'those responsible for the upheaval . . . despite the wealth of information available.'[144] His country offered the Director of Public Prosecutions legal assistance, but the offer was refused. In early December some of the hostage takers at Monasavu received suspended sentences.

Mara warned the Lau Provincial Council. 'The reconciliation that has been undertaken today will be worthless if investigations into the coup do not reveal the truth behind [its] staging.'[145] Many Fijians agreed, including the army's legal officer, Lieutenant Ilaisa Tagitupou. 'Justice was necessary', he said, 'because reconciliation was not appreciated.'[146] Interim Deputy Prime Minister, Ratu Epeli Nailatikau, took a more principled stand: 'Unadulterated greed and the unbelievable arrogance as was shamelessly displayed by chiefs and people alike on May 19 will not bring about paramountcy in this day and age.' Justice had to come before reconciliation, he declared, contradicting Qarase.[147]

But because Fijians could not agree on how to resolve the issues confronting them, the danger existed that they would simply try and muddle on without substantially changing anything. And that, some Fijians believed, carried the even greater risk of endless repetitions, endless violence, and endless misery. 'Unless we nip it now', stated one of the authors of the 1997 Constitution, Tomasi Vakatora, 'this mentality will continue.'[148]

In the wake of George Speight and Ilisoni Ligairi, Fijians faced a dilemma they could not resolve. Old ideas concerning paramountcy dictated that reconciliation among Fijians came before anything else. But reconciliation was never going to be possible until Fijians came to terms with their own diversity. And that meant understanding that the old politics of the *vanua* would no longer be enough to serve the new *vanua* and the international context in which it now existed.

To many chiefs such an understanding amounted to capitulation. When they met again in late April 2001, they signalled that they wanted more chiefs in a future Parliament and the level of debate in such a Parliament to reflect the status due to chiefs. Further, they wanted Fijian representation (perhaps nominated in the first instance by chiefs) restricted to provincial representation.[149] But Vanua Levu rebel Ratu Jo Dimuri disagreed. Provincial councils were captive to the Fijian chiefly elite and had long suppressed the voices of ordinary Fijians. They 'were to blame for the outbursts of Fijians' and should be replaced by *mataqali* (clan) and *yavusa* (district) meetings instead.[150]

Qarase, who desperately wanted to plug the gap left by Mara's departure and Rabuka's loss of power, had no time for such nonsense. Democracy, he warned, could be dangerous, especially if it undermined the very communal values that defined Fijian identity. Instead he proposed strengthening the chiefly system, granting $20 million to make the Great Council of Chiefs financially independent, making constitutional changes to place it under presidential rather than parliamentary control, and building the council its own administration complex.

Not surprisingly, the possibility of political consensus following the 2000 crisis threatened too many interests and too many power manoeuvres. Disunity generated its own self-serving momentum and rationalisations. It drove the Chief Justice to accept the army's abrogation of the Constitution and to deny legitimacy to anyone who questioned his judgment. It drove the Constitutional Review chairman, Asesela Ravuvu, to declare that 'politics must come before the law and legalities.' It drove Qarase to effectively argue that treason that succeeds is not treason.[151] And initially it drove Bainimarama to defend his abrogation, even when the High Court in November ruled it illegal and called for the reinstatement of the dismissed Parliament. 'It's no use moving towards democracy if we can't settle the security problem,' Bainimarama counselled.[152] But as Vakatora acknowledged, without democracy there is only dictatorship.[153]

By March 2001 Bainimarama appeared to agree. He accepted the Appeal Court's ruling that his actions in abrogating the Constitution had been illegal. So too did the Great Council of Chiefs, although reluctantly. It reappointed Iloilo as President and advised him to hold fresh elections under the 1997 Constitution. But having ended the threat of a commoner revolt in 2000, Fiji's elite had no wish to surrender to a Parliament where they did not control the power it had since gained. Consequently Iloilo now repeated – in Rabuka's words – Mara's 'kind of constitutionality'. He dismissed Chaudhry and appointed Momoedonu as Prime Minister. Once again Momoedonu advised the President to dissolve Parliament and then tendered his resignation. Qarase now returned as caretaker Prime Minister with the same Cabinet as before. So too did Ravuvu's Constitutional Review Committee, pursuing – according to the Citizens Constitutional Forum's Director, Rev Akuila Yabaki – the same 'illegal objective of George Speight'.[154]

Nothing, it seemed, had changed, except that all parties now agreed to an early election. Both Qarase and the President urged Fijians to unite behind one party. Only by this means could Fijian paramountcy be assured, meaning – as the new chair of the Great Council of Chiefs put it less delicately – that the Fijian establishment would not lose out as they had in 1999.[155]

But by mid-2001 the fallout from the coup seemed to have left Fiji even more divided politically than before. At the same time as the Great Council of Chiefs abandoned the SVT as its official party, rebel Macuata and Cakaudrove supporters split from the SVT to form a new Conservative Alliance Matanitu Vanua. Poseci Bune left the VLV to join PANU. PANU itself split, with Apisai Tora joining forces with Labour's Momoedonu to form a rival Bai Kei Viti (BKV). In May, deposed Deputy Prime Minister Tupeni Baba left the Labour Party to form his own party and join in a Moderate Fijian Coalition with Adi Kuini Vuikaba's FAP faction, Mick Beddoes' United Generals Party, and Rabuka. Rabuka appeared undecided in his loyalty to the SVT and later announced that he would not run in the August election. Even the precocious NVTLP had difficulty knowing what to do. It split, then re-united with its rival New National Party under a Taukei Civilian Forum. Melanesian members of the United Generals Party deserted the UGP, declaring themselves unhappy with their leader's support for the restoration of democracy.

Meanwhile, several provinces began forming their own parties (Naitasiri offered a Citizen's United Party) or proposed their own chiefs as provincial candidates, in both instances suggesting that no other Fijian candidates should challenge them. Lau put its weight behind Qarase, who in May launched his own Soqosoqo Duavata ni Lewenivanua (SDL or People's United Party), backed, it was alleged, by Fijian Holdings Limited[156] and supported by the Tailevu faction of the Fijian Association Party and eventually also by Naitasiri. Certainly many caretaker ministers and Qarase hoped the SDL would be their vehicle to success in elections forecast for August 2001. Even before the formation of his party, Qarase was on the campaign trail dispensing funds for roads and schools across the country. But like all other Fijian leaders, Qarase realised that much depended on how preferences were distributed. A government analysis of the 1999 election claimed that the SVT would have won had all Fijian parties directed preferences to it instead of the Labour Party.[157] Hence the rash of umbrella organisations formed – the Moderate Fijian Coalition, the Nationalists' Taukei Civilian Forum, and the SVT's Fijian Political Forum. In mid-May 2001 the Methodist Church attempted to bring together the rival coalitions by having all the major Fijian parties agree to share preferences and thus minimise the political consequences of division. But for the SVT the writing was on the wall. Whatever its goal in 2000, it was now no closer to government. Its alignment with extremists had prevented it seeking participation in a government of national unity in March 2001. It also created the opportunity for Qarase's SDL to seize moderate Fijian support. Once the extremists abandoned it, the SVT's strategies were in tatters. In June, Kubuabola stepped down as its leader.

Despite efforts to unite all Fijian parties under a single political umbrella, Fijians remained deeply divided over the meaning and the legality of the events of 2000. 'We have tried the illegal and unjust route on many occasions and we, the indigenous people, continue to pay the price for our recklessness,' warned lawyer Tupou Draunidalo towards the end of 2000. Her stepfather, Dr Timoci Bavadra, had been one of the May 1987 coup's first victims. 'History teaches us that arbitrary rule steadily diminishes public confidence in the legal system. The latter in turn inevitably leads to a state of anarchy.'

The ball, she believed, was now firmly in the hands of the military. 'Fiji will emerge from this mess when the FMF takes its role as the ultimate guardian of the State and Constitution more seriously. 'You reap what you sow',[158] she added. The Citizen's Constitutional Forum agreed. In May 2001 it legally challenged the President's failure to recall Parliament in March.[159] Qarase dismissed its members as 'zealots of constitutionality' and declared that 'the welfare of people come before the rule of law'.[160] Pressure was placed on the CCF. It was deregistered as a charitable trust. When its case eventually came before Suva's High Court, Justice Scott ruled that the President had acted legally under the Doctrine of Necessity. The CCF's barrister, Sir Vijay Singh, declared the judgement 'a terrorist charter to any group wishing to destabilise a government'[161]; its legacy for Fiji —government by the gun. But the pressure told on the Chief Justice. He announced his intention to resign after the election. The President also felt the heat. When the Lautoka High Court upheld a Labour Party writ seeking the Constitutional Review Committee's dismissal, he disbanded it in July for the second time.

The events of 2000 demonstrated above all the disunity that had always existed within Fijian society but which, in the past, had been successfully glossed over by its colonial remaking and by constant references to Indian threats. Both the 1990 and 1997 constitutions gave Fijians ultimate authority over their country. Why, then, had Fijians got it so wrong? What had happened in the past to distort so their quest for self-determination, and how did that past now shape their solution to the Fijian question?

Chapter 2

Indigenous nationalism and the quest for Fijian paramountcy

THE INDIGENOUS FIJIANS

Fijians originated from today's southern China. For more than 3,000 years waves of migration swept down through South-East Asia and fanned out across the Pacific. In time the three major ethnic groupings of the Pacific region – Melanesia, Polynesia and Micronesia – emerged. Travel led to inter-mixing, especially in Fiji, which sits between Melanesia and Polynesia. Here trade and strategic alliances meant that few communities developed in isolation from each other. However, being the product of at least three main waves of migrants, as well as more recent settlers from Tonga, Fiji possessed cultural diversity long before the arrival of Europeans.

To the early Europeans a striking feature of Fijian society was the warfare between tribal groups. By introducing firearms and forming alliances with already prominent Fijian communities, the Europeans believed they could influence outcomes. Influential European settlers tried to establish a national government under the *Vunivalu* Ratu Seru Cakobau, a paramount chief from Bau, a tiny island off the Tailevu coast not far from today's capital, Suva. Cakobau had his own ambitions. He wanted to be chief of all Fiji (*Tui Viti*).

But the national government collapsed, and in 1874 a harried Cakobau signed the Deed of Cession to Britain.

Not all Fijians accepted the handover to Britain, and at various times openly rebelled against their colonial masters and their mainly eastern Fijian allies. Colonial rule brought a new order to the islands but failed to end the dynamic system of alliances and rivalries, which continue to shape Fijian communities to this day.

Before contact with Europeans, then, Fiji was composed of small and relatively autonomous societies established by migrant peoples who had fought, traded and married among themselves for a long time. How were these small and relatively autonomous societies organised? What were their traditions? What were their key social values? We pose these questions because they are important for a better understanding of the debate and challenges that confront the indigenous question today. And in large part the debate continues because of disagreements over precisely the questions we pose. This is true of Fijians themselves and that, in turn, is the result of their historical diversity, differences and fluidity. In short, there is no such thing as a single, homogenous, unchanging Fijian culture. There were many Fijian cultures across which there certainly were similarities, but there were significant differences as well.

In this regard, the single most important feature of British colonial rule was its attempt to impose on Fijian cultural diversity a homogeneity and uniformity that previously did not exist. Out of that attempt emerged what, for many people, became the received wisdom on Fijian tradition and identity. But the attempt was only partly successful and the way was left open for differing views on what the past was like and therefore for selective interpretations to suit particular interests and agendas. Therein lies the origin of the continuing debate about Fijian culture and tradition. It explains how and why some people today, including Fijians, use terms like 'Fijian', 'Fijian culture' and 'Fijian tradition' as if these are homogenous categories. In so doing, they take a particular but contestable view of Fiji's past and they do this because it advances their interests and agendas. So what, then, is the received wisdom about Fijians, Fijian culture and Fijian tradition?

The organisation of Fijian societies varied and this, along with other differences, posed a major problem for the British colonial administration, one of whose first tasks was to ensure social control. But order would be more possible with uniformity, and that did not exist. Sir Arthur Gordon, the first governor, therefore set about imposing uniformity by constructing his own version of traditional Fijian society. In time it became the received wisdom, and is as follows.

The primary social unit was *i tokatoka*, family groupings. Related *i tokatoka* combined to form *mataqali,* which the colonial authorities defined as the primary division of the village. All the village *mataqali* formed a *yavusa* and various *yavusa* within particular localities combined to form a wider political unit, *vanua*. But the term *vanua* also has a much broader meaning. It also refers to the collective body politic and the relationship of the people to the land. The collective sense of identity this signifies is captured by the word *vakavanua,* which literally means 'the way of the land'.

Sense of place was therefore enormously important. People lived in the village (*koro*) but the primary unit to which they belonged determined their place in the wider social structure. It was the basis for the individual's sense of attachment and identification, so that, although commoners deferred to their chief, their primary attachment was to the group.

Fijian societies were hierarchical but, as with the form of social organisation, there were significant differences between the social hierarchies. In the western parts of Fiji, for example, the hierarchy was flatter than in the east. Also, social hierarchies were not static or immutable. They evolved. For example, only in the nineteenth century in some parts of Fiji did the position of *vunivalu* (military chief, because of his military power) acquire higher status than that of *Roko Tui* (high chief). In general, however, the pattern of social hierarchies was as follows.

Chiefs occupied the highest level of the social ladder. 'Paramount' chiefs were at the very top, below them were lower-ranking ones. Commoners occupied the lower levels and individual status was determined by three major factors: occupation, age and gender. Some occupations, for example, chiefly spokesmen (*matanivanua*), priests (*bete*) and warriors (*bati*) had higher status than artisans. The vast majority of commoners, who bore the primary burden of producing the needs of the society, were at the bottom of the pecking order. Status and authority also came with age; minors deferred to elders. And finally, men were dominant over women. Fijian societies were, and remain, patriarchal.

In this kind of situation, it is not surprising that there was a very strong sense of place, and that social behaviour was highly regulated. From a very young age, Fijians learned what was expected of them. This happened within the family and at the many occasions that brought people together – births, marriages, deaths, inter-village gatherings, political events and so on – and such occasions were typically highly ritualised.

In these sorts of ways, key social values were reinforced and the pressure to conform maintained. Three social values are especially important for understanding the problems that continue to beset Fijians today because appeals to these are made in pursuit of the nationalist agenda. One is the primacy of the group over the individual.

Group welfare and harmony were paramount and instilling a strong sense of place and belonging in individuals was hugely important. Through socialisation they learned the rules of behaviour and requirements of protocol, and these were constantly reaffirmed through ritual. Conformity and compliance were vital and were rewarded through various means: acknowledgement, acclaim and other positive forms of reinforcement. Precocity, pretentiousness and wayward behaviour were frowned upon and penalised. Direct forms of punishment included beating and death; indirect but no less effective forms included gossip, ridicule and social ostracism.

The importance of group primacy was also reflected in Fijians' relationship to land. Land occupied a central place in the Fijian way of life. It provided material needs, had enormous spiritual significance and was owned by the group, either the *i tokatoka* or the *mataqali*, not the individual. European settlers introduced the concept of private property, and before long much of the best land was in their hands. But the vast majority of land remained in Fijian hands and today Fijians still own more than 83 per cent of the total.

Arthur Gordon legalised group ownership. Significantly, one of his successors, Everard im Thurn, tried to overturn this. He believed that Fijian advancement could never be secured so long as Fijians were hamstrung by a system of land tenure that was not based on individual ownership. Accordingly, between 1905 and 1909, he passed legislation to correct this. Back in London, a shocked Arthur Gordon launched a stinging attack against im Thurn's experiment and he eventually won the day. The relevant legislation was repealed. Group ownership of land became legally entrenched as a form of proprietary rights.

Individual property rights and group property rights were, of course, in fundamental conflict. It was obvious that administrative problems would arise. One way to deal with this was to shift much of the burden of administering group ownership of land to a 'separate' system of administration — the system of native administration, which we describe later — and within it prime responsibility for this task fell to the Native Lands Trust Board (NLTB).

Because Fijian land is group-owned, banks would not lend against it. The choice for most Fijians, therefore, was either to keep their land for subsistence purposes or to lease it. Many chose the latter option. For many Fijians, therefore, cash income came largely in the form of rent. But the vast majority of ordinary Fijians benefited little from land rents, and still do not. Fifty per cent of rental income goes to the Native Land Trust Board and the chiefly elite. The rest is shared among the large number of commoners, with the result that each person receives very little. Little wonder that this has long been a sore point with many commoners. They have, of course, voiced their discontent, mainly in private but occasionally in public, but little has changed. This speaks volumes about their relative powerlessness and the enduring culture of deference and obedience by which they are bound. This is not to suggest, however, that there are no limits to deference and obedience. A good recent example is the assertiveness and defiance shown in 2000 by landowners around the hydro-electric power station in the interior of Viti Levu. Their bid for compensation was successful.

Another key social value is generosity. Because group welfare was paramount, individual members had a strong social obligation not only to help others but also to contribute to community needs. The pressure to give was enormous, and people were expected not only to be generous but also to be seen to be generous. Fijians hate being called *mamaqi*, which means selfish or stingy. But being generous was relatively easy in the old days. Gifts or borrowings of food, mats, clothing and so on were largely possible because supplies were generally good or could be produced fairly quickly. Colonialism changed this, however. Private property, individualism, the money economy, paid employment, formal education and consumerism brought new pressures and created new needs and aspirations.

Before long the Fijian need for money grew, but limited employment and economic opportunities meant there was usually insufficient money to meet individual and family needs, let alone meet social obligations. Rising prices did not help, and in time Fijian customary obligations became more costly and burdensome. Yet the pressure to give, and give generously, remains strong to this day — and the consequences are profound. As we shall see later, this is often cited as one reason for Fijian business failure.

Three other points about generosity are worth making. The first is that generosity was a two-way thing. Giving carried the expectation that others would in turn be generous to the giver. Unfortunately this did not always happen. Second, the pressure to be generous was great on Fijians who remained in their places of origin but much less so on those who migrated elsewhere. By leaving, the latter left behind mechanisms of support that village life offered, but neither were they as bound by village obligations. One important consequence was that migrants were forced to make it on their own in their new milieu. That usually meant acquiring new knowledge, skills and experience. In many instances this produced greater success, which often became the source of envy of Fijians back in the village. In a real sense, this is just another version of Fijian envy of other migrant peoples, including Indians. Third, generosity has been exploited, especially in recent times, as a means of raising capital for investment through the practice of community collection called *soli vakavanua*. The problem there is that returns from investment were not distributed fairly. We will come back to this later.

A third traditional value of immense consequence is deference to authority. Chiefs, men and elders were the main authorities. They commanded respect and expected obedience. They talked, others listened; they commanded, others followed. Interactions between superiors and subordinates were governed by strict protocol.

Subordinates adopted deferential forms of demeanour and speech. Correct demeanour included keeping an appropriate distance, avoiding eye contact, a seated or slightly crouched position and a bowed head. Soft-spokenness, respectful forms of address and unhurried discussions were also the norm. Superior rank and status had to be acknowledged, even if only indirectly, before getting to the point of the discussion. And the main point had to be made in a respectful way. Modesty and self-efface-ment were expected; assertiveness and self-promotion discouraged; and care taken not to cause offence, especially where sensitive matters were involved. Disagreement was best handled in private rather than in public. Consensus and quiet diplomacy were preferred over an adversarial style. Criticism was to be as gentle, muted or elliptical as possible. For people not schooled in these ways, especially foreigners, the scope for misinter-pretation and misunderstanding was considerable, and this is still the case today.

But this general account needs qualification. Deference did not neces-sarily mean total subservience, acceptance or agreement. Commoners deferred but, equally, chiefs were expected to listen to their people. Failure to do so carried the risk of resistance, even rebellion and displacement. Chiefs certainly had authority, but they were not the final arbiters. Decisions were made on the basis of consultation and consensus. Unilateral or arbi-trary decisions by chiefs could make the people unhappy and restless, a situation that is captured by the Fijian saying, *e kudru na lewenivanua* (the people are grumbling). Chiefs ignored this at their peril.

On the other hand, how the people felt was not always clear, and this remains true today. As Qarikau, general manager of the NLTB, recently pointed out, 'Indigenous Fijians lag behind because when chiefly political leaders arrive at their villages, their people agree to everything they say without question.'[1] The danger here is that appearance can be mistaken for reality. Agreement in public can be misleading. It does not necessarily reflect private feelings.

With this important qualification in mind, the norms of behaviour described above may have been good for conformity and order, but they did not engender an open and enquiring culture. The scope for critical thinking and free exchange of views was severely limited. Stymied by the weight of authority and received wisdom, and constricted by convention, there was little room for the expression of independent thought and the development of skills of argumentation.

With the arrival of Europeans, this culture of deference and restraint became rather more complex because Fijians were soon expected to defer also to their new economic, technological and political superiors: the governor, district commissioner, judge, policeman, employer, and so on. And there was no shortage of daily reminders of the new authority: the Bible, the British flag and anthem, the judge's wig, and so on. But old and new authorities were often in conflict and for Fijians this was often a cause of discomfort. Tradition pulled one way, colonialism the other, and the situation became even more complicated over time as more and more Fijians, commoners included, acquired the new authority in their positions as public servants, parliamentarians, judges, employers, and so on. The contradictions between older and newer roles thus became a headache for Fijians and often caused them to behave in ways that might seem odd and even led to wrong impressions.

This overview of Fijian societies in the past is, of course, sketchy and selective and we readily acknowledge their many positive and exemplary aspects, especially caring and mutual support. This is true even in relation to the chiefs, who were not only rulers, but guardians of the common good as well. Their primary obligation was to ensure the welfare of the group; they too had to show caring. It is not surprising, therefore, that Fijians had the same expectation of their colonial masters, who duly set about the task of convincing the natives that they did care. The problem was that the colonists decided they knew what was best for the natives. For a long time, many natives believed them.

One of the first tasks that confronted the first governor, Sir Arthur Gordon, was to contain any potential indigenous threat to colonial rule. He knew he needed chiefly support to control the Fijian masses. In his words, only through them could Fiji be 'most peaceably, cheaply and easily governed'.[2] But there was another consideration. The Fijians, he believed, were incapable of coping with the rigours of modern civilisation and therefore needed protection until they were ready for the modern world. Indirect rule through a separate system of native administration was the way to do this.

Gordon was troubled by regional variations in social structure, despite the fundamental similarities, so he set about constructing his own model of 'the traditional social structure' and used it as the basis of the system of native administration that he duly set in place. In 1948 his Native Administration became the Fijian Administration and later, after independence in 1970, the Ministry of Fijian Affairs.

A leading scholar described the system of native administration in this way: 'Whatever outward semblance of a traditional or indigenous system Gordon's native administration possessed for European observers, Fijians clearly regarded it as an imported institution directly under the control of the Governor.'[3] Nevertheless, it became an integral part of the colonial regime and in time Fijians were increasingly won over to it. The reason for its acceptance was in no small measure due to the enormous influence of the most senior Fijian in the colonial administration during the early and mid-twentieth century, Ratu (later Sir) Lala Sukuna (*Tui Lau*), Oxford-educated, and commonly regarded as 'the statesman of Fiji'.

At the apex of the Native Administration was the Council of Chiefs, entirely a creation of Gordon. No such institution previously existed. A purely advisory body, it nonetheless came to be regarded as the very embodiment of the Fijian body politic, not surprisingly largely as a result of chiefly efforts. Today, the successor to the Council of Chiefs, the Great Council of

Chiefs (*Bose Levu Vakaturaga*) is similarly regarded. In recent years, however, a small but increasing number of Fijians, including prominent ones, have begun to question its place and role.

Nonetheless, the establishment of the Council of Chiefs as a centralised guardian of their interests provided a new means for Fijians to more resolutely defend their affairs whenever they felt them threatened by the activities of colonial authorities or migrant Indians. That role we pursue later, but first, a final note on the question: 'Who are the indigenous Fijians?'

One answer to the question 'who is Fijian?' is 'whoever is registered in the Fijian Register, the *Vola ni Kawa Bula* (VKB)'. The colonial government created this register to help define land ownership. In many respects the VKB mocked the traditions of Fijians. They had always been a very receptive people and ancestry had little to do with being Fijian. Certainly there existed no tradition of exclusivity in becoming Fijian.[4] But by the late twentieth century, many nationalists saw the register as a means to impose exclusivity. They did not want Fijians diluted by outsiders and reduced 'to a pitiful race of beggars'.[5]

Who gets on to the VKB, and how? First, individuals have to register. This usually happens soon after birth. Second, the offspring of Fijian parents automatically qualify. Third, the *mataqali* to which individuals are said to belong must be identified. Fourth, individuals of part-Fijian ancestry may qualify if they are accepted by the nominated *mataqali*. Usually this is simply a matter for families — *i tokatoka* — to determine. They decide who they want to accept as family members and who they do not. But outside of the family, acceptance may be subject to entirely different considerations. And undoubtedly one of the contributing influences is the very rigid system of racial classification introduced to Fiji during colonialism and sustained for political and social reasons ever since.

No better example of the sensitivity that surrounds identity can found in the way Fijians view and treat 'mixed race' people. In Fijian custom, there is a special relationship between uncles and their sisters' children. It is called *vasu*. It is telling that Fijians typically consider many part-Fijians with European ancestry as *vasu* and, accordingly, treat them very much as close relatives. Because Europeans held special privileges in Fiji in the past, Fijians obviously saw advantages in giving them special status. Fijians had always treated outsiders in this way, Tongans being a classic example. This is not always as true of their relationship with other part-Fijians during and after the colonial period, in particular Solomon Islanders and Chinese. Worse affected were those of Indian ancestry.

The case of Jim Ah Koy reveals the level of disunity among Fijians on this issue. Of Fijian and Chinese ancestry, Ah Koy is one of Fiji's leading businessmen and a former senior cabinet minister. After the 1987 coups he declared himself Fijian on the basis of his registration in the VKB. The case sparked much debate and joking about who is Fijian and, very importantly, who is entitled to the benefits that only Fijians enjoy. But the final word came from Ah Koy's chief: 'If the *Yavusa* Naibati wants [his registration] who else under the sun should complain.'[6] Ah Koy's case is only one example of many mixed-race people who sought to identify themselves as Fijian. Another recent case is George Speight's father, Sam, registered in the VKB as Savenaca Tokainavo.

But even the greater acceptance and affection accorded to some part-Fijians does not diminish the fact that for many Fijians during and after colonialism, mixed-race people are just that. They are not real or 'full' Fijians. From the English term 'half-caste', Fijians derived the generic *kai loma* to describe mixed-race people. It literally means 'belonging in the middle' and is sometimes used to drive home to the *kai loma* the point that they are 'not really Fijian' and therefore do not really belong. A common put-down is '*kai loma, e sega na nomu qele*', which means 'you half-caste, you have no land'. But it is also said of Fijians that when they want something from mixed-race people they affectionately called them *vasu*. When displeased, they call them *kai loma*.

Of course, these generalisations fail to distinguish the differing reactions of families, *mataqali* and other groupings. Nonetheless, such sentiments underline Fijian sensitivity about their identity, and their touchiness is all the greater because being a Fijian definitely has its benefits. Certainly there are traditional obligations (paying village dues, for example) but there are also traditional entitlements (access to land, for example). Especially prized, however, are the contemporary entitlements that come in various forms of special treatment – preferential loans, dedicated scholarships and import quota allocations and, as happened after the May 1987 coup, senior official and political positions set aside exclusively for Fijians.

To some extent these new privileges made necessary more precise definitions of Fijianness. Pacific Islanders, who had previously been regarded electorally as Fijians, were suddenly deemed to be non-Fijians in 1990. In 1992 nationalists tried – unsuccessfully – to excise mixed-race Fijians from the VKB.

Given their inability to define Fijianness with any precision, Fijians were unlikely to reach any consensus on a common name for all Fiji citizens, particularly if any proposed national name threatened in any way their exclusive identity as Fijians. Consequently the debate over a national name has been protracted. In 1995 Sitiveni Rabuka reopened the debate in a special New Year address.

> For too long we have kept our society fragmented by concentrating too much on our racial origins. We look upon ourselves as Fijians, as Indians, part-Europeans, Chinese, Pacific Islanders. A country that does not have an encompassing identity for its citizens will always be incomplete. I have concluded, after much searching of my conscience, that it is time for us to become 'Fijians'. I will repeat that – all citizens of Fiji should be known as Fijian.[7]

But he was unsuccessful in effecting change. When the 1997 Constitution finally proclaimed a national name, it chose Fiji Islander. It is not a name that, by any stretch of the imagination, won universal acclaim. But for many Fijians it is acceptable because the term Fijian now refers exclusively to indigenous Fijians. Which leaves the matter of the Rotumans to be explained.

Rotuma is a small Polynesian island 800 km to the north of the main islands of Fiji. Not long after colonising Fiji, Britain annexed Rotuma as part of Fiji. Rotumans are very small in number but, as an indigenous people, have a special place in Fiji. They are not listed in the VKB but are accorded many of the special privileges enjoyed by indigenous Fijians – loans, scholarships and so on. And as with Fijian culture and tradition, theirs too is protected under the current and previous Constitutions. But two points about Rotumans. First, those who live on the main islands of Fiji are migrants but are treated much better than other migrant groups, especially Indians. Second, the special treatment accorded Rotumans is often questioned. Some Fijians resent it. For the purposes of this book, the indigenous question relates only to the indigenous Fijians.

There is one final aspect to Fijianness that we should note. As Fiji becomes increasingly urbanised (48 per cent by 2000), many of the older associations with Fijianness are becoming less relevant. When in 1992 Fijian nationalists insisted on registration in the VKB as the precondition for voting as a Fijian, they were shocked to discover that nearly one-fifth of the Fijian population had never bothered to have themselves registered in the VKB.[8]

However, this did not lessen a growing sense among many Fijians that collectively they were disadvantaged, in particular by Indians. We turn now to explore why and how they came to see themselves as threatened.

FIJIAN PERCEPTIONS OF THE THREAT OF INDIAN DOMINATION

Europeans changed Fiji profoundly. They brought capitalism, Christianity, new systems of education and law, new forms of media, and all the values and symbols that go with these. These forces were never allowed totally free rein but the British, and Gordon in particular, took the view that because Fijians were only just emerging from a state of savage barbarism they needed protection and nurturing until they were ready to cope with the rigours of modernity. Keeping them under a system of native administration was the way to do this.

The underlying assumption was that development in Fiji could proceed on the basis of separate development of ethnic groups. That assumption, which continues to this day, is fundamentally flawed and a major reason for the problems that beset Fiji's development strategy generally and the indigenous question in particular. In short, Fiji's development path has failed a great many Fijians. The problem is that they wrongly identified the real causes of their predicament. In reality the colonial path of development, and not Indians, threatened their interests.

There is a history of Fijian resistance against European domination – social, political and economic – but superior European power, with the help of native collusion (especially by eastern chiefs), won out. Rebellious elements were crushed, agitators suppressed and critics silenced. The task of containment was all the easier because opposition was small, dispersed and unorganised, and most Fijians submitted to the emerging new order. They converted to Christianity, covered up their bodies, embraced new forms of education, obeyed colonial law and increasingly engaged in the capitalist economy – mainly as workers, buyers and sellers.

Winning over Fiji hearts and minds was helped a great deal by the Europeans' powers of persuasion. Persuasive Europeans, who projected themselves as having Fijian interests at heart, negated Fijian fears of being overrun by the white man. Conveniently for the Europeans, many Fijians believed them. They believed them even more after the arrival of Indians; they became the substitute 'threat to the Fijian race'.

Sugar production was the backbone of the colonial economy. The major producer was an Australian company, the Colonial Sugar Refining Company (CSR), but there were local European planters as well. Attempts to coax Fijians to work in the canefields were not very successful, and Governor Arthur Gordon, drawing on his experience in Trinidad and Mauritius, turned to India as a source of cheap labour. He introduced to Fiji a system of indentured labour under which labourers were imported from India on five-year contracts. The system lasted from 1879 to 1916 and brought in 60,595 Indians.

The Indian migrants came from a number of widely differing provinces, in particular the northern Uttar Pradesh and the southern Tamil Nadu. They did not arrive as a singular or united Indian people. Ethnicity, religion, caste, place of origin, and language divided them. What transcended those divisions for the settlers were their colonial experiences. It created a new unifying identity for them as Indo Fijians. Thus a new racial dynamic began in Fiji, with consequences which continue to this day.

Indentured Indians toiled under atrocious conditions and at the end of their contracts were offered the option of returning to India or remaining in Fiji. Many chose to remain and from as early as 1884 they were presented with the opportunity of becoming sugarcane farmers rather than continuing as mere labourers.

Not long after setting up in Fiji, CSR realised that the most profitable area of sugar production was in milling and so decided to concentrate its efforts there. It hoped that local European planters would be able to provide an adequate supply of cane, but they were unable to do so. As a result, CSR developed its own plantations on a much larger scale than originally intended and before long began leasing parts of its estates to local Europeans. From 1894 it began leasing small plots of land to Indians who had completed their indenture. This had important effects.

With Indians now rival cane suppliers, local European farmers saw Indians as a threat to their interests. Anti-Indian sentiment soon emerged. As one writer put it, 'This rise of the Indian canefarmer was a pointer to the future of Fiji. To the planters, the unindentured Indian was a potential competitor, who picked the eyes out of the land available for leasing.'[9] But by the mid-1930s the CSR small farm system had become firmly established as the basis for the sugar industry, and the majority of cane farmers were Indians.

By then, too, new waves of free migrants from India had intensified anti-Indian sentiment among Europeans. These new migrants from Gujarat and the Punjab increasingly engaged in business and the professions. Sacrifice, hard work and dedication to education were key factors in their success, but the more they achieved the more that antagonism towards them grew. Local Europeans feared and resented the challenge to their commercial and professional dominance and mounted a sustained rearguard action that was highly effective because it was racist. By projecting Indians as a threat to the Fijian people, the European community was able to hide the real cause of their concerns.

For their part, many Fijians sided readily with the Europeans. Having languished under a system of native administration that was supposed to 'protect' them but which in reality left them further and further behind other ethnic groups, they were susceptible to racist sentiments and stereotypes, often initiated by Europeans. Indians were said to be individualistic, ambitious, scheming and manipulative. They were also *mamaqi*. It did not help their image that their strong anti-colonialism was portrayed as traitorous during World War II and compared unfavourably with Fijian military participation.

When members of the growing Indian business and professional elite agitated for political representation and greater political rights generally, local Europeans cast them as agitators and upstarts. They resisted the idea of equal representation for all races and orchestrated Fijian opposition as well. In 1922, for example, a leading hotelier, J.J. Ragg, wrote to a chief urging that he 'endeavour to permeate the whole of the Fijian race with the fixed idea that the granting of the franchise and equal status to the Indians in Fiji would mean the ultimate loss of all their land and rights, and later their final extinction from the face of the earth'.[10]

The alleged threat of Fijian extinction appeared more real because of demographic changes. In 1911 Fijians accounted for 62 per cent of the population, Indians 29 per cent. By 1936, the figures had changed to 50 per cent and 43 per cent. Ten years later, Indians were the majority and their growth rate was higher than that of Fijians. Local Europeans were worried about competition from Indian businesses and, wishing to restore their economic pre-eminence, used the demographic shift to strengthen their alliance with the Fijian elite and attack Indians.[11]

On 16 July 1946, A.A. Ragg, also a member of the prominent hotelling family, triggered a debate of enormous significance when he tabled the following motion in the Legislative Council:

That in the opinion of this Council the time has arrived – in view of the great increase in the non-Fijian inhabitants and its consequential political development – to emphasise the terms of the Deed of Cession to assure that the interests of the Fijian race are safeguarded and a guarantee given that Fiji is to be preserved and kept as a Fijian country for all time.[12]

Speaking to his motion, Ragg launched a highly provocative and inflammatory broadside against Indians. These 'aliens', he said, had 'no responsibility under the Deed of Cession'. The Europeans, on the other hand, were 'co-trustees with the Imperial Government in the Deed of Cession in the care that should be given to the native race'. On this, there was to be no room for doubt: 'The duty of trusteeship devolves upon Europeans and in this duty the Indians have no part.' Interestingly, he also had words for Fijians:

[C]haracter is just what the natives have not. We who work for and among them know, too painfully, how deficient in all manly qualities they are. Courage, honour, firmness, pure ambition, truthfulness, unselfishness – these and kindred qualities are all too rare . . . they mean well, but being deficient in character they are weak and the victims of circumstances.[13]

No Fijian member of the Council challenged his open effrontery so dominant was the European community. In fact, a Fijian member (a chief) seconded Ragg's motion and another (also a chief) had this to say:

[T]his motion as it stands concerns the future well-being of my people, who are likely to be overwhelmed or swamped by this Colossus of Indian domination in this Colony. This problem . . . must be solved before it is too late . . . I support the motion.

Another chief even lavished Ragg with praise:

I support this motion because to my knowledge it is the first time for many years that someone has had the courage to table and speak on a motion of this kind.[14]

This was a momentous debate. It was an official and public affirmation of the 'paramountcy of Fijian interests' and it confirmed an opinion already widely held in private among Europeans and Fijians – that the Fijian people were under threat from 'Indian domination'. How real was this threat?

Certainly Indians were now the majority and, yes, they were pushing for equal political rights. But the suggestion that they would become politically dominant was simply not borne out by the facts. The most glaring of these was the stout European and Fijian resistance to the Indian call for a single electoral roll. What later emerged was separate electoral rolls for Fijians, Indians and 'Others' (who were called General Electors). With the electorate divided racially, and the alliance between Fijians and Europeans so strong, Indian political domination was never likely.

On the economic side, no convincing evidence was given of Indian domination, or of its likelihood. It is true that Indians were visibly prominent in various economic sectors, especially retail, transport and manufacturing, but visibility and preponderance are not the same as economic dominance. The vast majority of Indian cane farmers had small farms and were not wealthy by any stretch of the imagination. The most profitable sector of the sugar industry, milling, was dominated by the foreign CSR which, in 1973, sold its interest to the government.

The other major economic sectors were also dominated by Australian companies: Emperor Gold Mines; Morris Hedstrom (retailing); and the Bank of New South Wales (later Westpac), ANZ Bank and Queensland Insurance. Tourism, which local Europeans planned to dominate, did not take off until the mid-1960s. It, too, was foreign-dominated, especially the most profitable area—accommodation. The commercial fishing and timber industries did not emerge until the 1970s and foreign companies or the government also dominated them.[15] As for the public sector, it is true that during the colonial period Indians held the largest proportion of jobs there, including many senior ones, but that too eventually changed.

Together these sectors accounted for the bulk of the formal, non-subsistence economy. The key point here is that the facts simply did not square with the so-called threat of Indian economic domination. Nor did they demonstrate the myth that Indians were the cause of Fijian economic disadvantage. What they did reveal is that some Indians, especially Gujeratis, were prominent in the economy and some profited at the expense of Fijians. But they were a minority and, what is more, some of them were allied with the Fijian elite. The talk of 'Indian domination' therefore lumped all Indians together as if they were a united community that had the same interests. This was not so then and it is not the case now. But perceptions, fuelled by the visibility and large number of Indian businesses and professionals, were important. As long as Fijians believed the talk, the threat was as good as real. And it had to be countered.

COUNTERING THE THREAT WITH 'FIJIAN PARAMOUNTCY'

The general strategy to counter the threat of 'eventual Indian domination' was based on the notion of Fijian paramountcy. But what precisely this meant was not altogether clear, and is not still. Indeed, the term itself is quite misleading because it lumps all Fijians together as if they are the same and have the same interests. They do not. Certainly there are common bonds and shared interests but, as in the past, there are divisions and conflicting interests as well. The fundamental split is a class division between the elites on the one hand and the poor and disadvantaged on the other; and cutting across this are tribal, provincial and regional splits. It has always suited the Fijian elite to hide their class interests behind the rhetoric of Fijian interests and paramountcy and to blame the predicament of ordinary Fijians on others – namely the Indians.

In terms of particular strategies adopted to counter Fijian perceptions of threat, efforts at preserving Fijian culture and tradition are important. Fijian education has long been a central plank of government policy. The curriculum and the establishment of separate schools for Fijians were avenues for the further inculcation of Fijian culture. Significantly, some schools were established for the education of children of the Fijian elite. The two best-known are Adi Cakobau School (ACS) for girls and Queen Victoria School

(QVS) for boys. Many of the present Fijian elite are former students of these schools. The church was another key institution. There, religious practice was infused with Fijian cultural practice. Social organisations – village groups, sports clubs, women's organisations and so on – were also important in keeping a distinct Fijian culture alive.

Sitting astride all these was the Fijian Administration. Its precursor, the Native Administration, had gone through pretty testing times. Cost-cutting by the Colonial Government and growing criticism by local Europeans led to constant reviews and changes in the system of native administration. In 1917 the Suva-based Department of Native Administration was abolished and further reviews and reorganisations followed in the 1920s and 1930s. This sustained attack threatened, above all else, the interests of the emergent, chief-dominated Fijian bureaucratic class. Their appeals against the assault were couched not in terms of their threatened class interests but in terms of a threat to the interests of Fijians as a race. The Fijian elite realised very early that its interests as a class were best protected by presenting their class problems as problems of Fijians as a whole. This strategy eventually bore fruit, especially as the Fijian elite had helped in the suppression of the Viti Kabani movement, a commoner struggle led by a Fijian carpenter called Apolosi Ranawai during and after World War I.

A major reorganisation led to the formation of a new Fijian Administration in 1948, largely independent from central government. Its own Fijian-controlled provincial and district finances and a Fijian Affairs Board (FAB) controlled administrative affairs and made regulations that governed the lives of Fijians.[16]

At the bottom of its administrative hierarchy were district councils; above them the provincial councils. At the apex was the Council (later Great Council) of Chiefs, the operating arm of which was the FAB. The conservatism of the board, as a scholar of Fijian affairs put it, 'reflected its domination by a political elite of chiefs linked as a multiplex group by kin or affinal ties, and by associations in the Council of Chiefs and Legislative Council'.[17] Fijian members of the Legislative Council served as senior bureaucrats in the Fijian Administration and often also held office in other state agencies.

The fledgling Fijian bureaucratic class, for so long under serious threat, had finally ensured its survival. In the years ahead its chiefly members would be joined by commoners and the strategy of presenting its class interests as the interests of Fijians as a race would serve them well. Indeed, this strategy became the linchpin for the protection of the interests of the Fijian elite as a whole – bureaucratic, political and economic – and therein lies the ideological basis of 'Fijian paramountcy'. Behind the talk and rhetoric of Fijian paramountcy lay its hidden driving force – the protection of Fijian elite interests.

With a stronger Fijian Administration, expectations were high that the plight of ordinary Fijians would improve. Their economic condition was particularly worrying and the 1950s brought few signs of real improvement. 'Subsistence affluence', preference for the 'leisurely' village lifestyle, lack of entrepreneurship and capitalist discipline, communalistic as opposed to individualistic values, pressures from traditional obligations, educational under-achievement and lack of capital were identified as obstacles. But several major investigations pointed the finger also at the Fijian Administration.

A 1959 enquiry into the 'economic problems and prospects of the Fijian people' identified the root causes as the communal system and the Fijian Administration, both having been 'designed for non-economic ends'.[18] A year later a commissioned report on the 'natural resources and population of the colony' took the same view. It was in no doubt about what should happen to the Fijian Administration. '[It is] an unnecessary expense which Fiji cannot afford . . . and should not continue for any longer than is absolutely necessary.'[19]

Yet another investigation concluded that 'the effects of the Fijian Administration on the economic growth of the Fijian people have been little short of disastrous, and the source of much of the difficulty lies within the structure and philosophy of the Administration as a political unit'. Its appointments 'leaned heavily on the side of family position and benign paternal, even, aristocratic authority'. More generally, it tended to 'lean on autocratic authority and to exercise it arbitrarily and sometimes capriciously'.[20] Strong stuff, but it struck a chord with a growing number of disgruntled

Fijians. Their own administrative structure had failed to improve change to their lot. It stifled the progress of those it was meant to serve.

A further review and yet more changes in the 1960s loosened the administrative straitjacket. There was now more talk also, about the need to promote greater individualism and economic competitiveness among Fijians, and various agricultural schemes became the primary vehicle for Fijian economic advancement. But these schemes continued to fail. Moreover, geared as it was to the rural sector, the Fijian Administration was incapable of responding adequately to new Fijian economic aspirations. By the mid-1960s the economic boom was not in agriculture but in tourism, commerce, building, transportation and the state sector. Fijians wanted a piece of the action. But how to achieve this? The answer would not be found in the Fijian Administration but in new political and ideological arenas – political because it had to do with Fijian state power, and ideological because it entailed a total reversal of the ideology (though not the practice) of racialism.

In 1960 leaders of the Indian community formed the Federation Party. High on the Party's agenda was the continuing call for political equality, a common electoral roll and independence from Britain. The local European community and the Fijian leadership resisted any talk of independence and attacked Indians for encouraging it. By 1962, however, independence struggles throughout the British colonial empire had gathered momentum and in Fiji the signs from the Colonial Government were that constitutional change was likely. The Fijian leadership's response was simply to insist that should Britain withdraw, then control should be given to Fijians. But this did not necessarily mean that it now favoured independence. Its position had to be clarified and during 1962 the recently-formed and leading Fijian political organisation, the Fijian Association, convened a series of meetings to discuss the matter. At the end of the year it reaffirmed its opposition to independence. Local Europeans supported them and together they attacked Indians for their pro-independence stance.

Why was the Fijian leadership so opposed to independence? Essentially because of its general weakness. It lacked economic clout, it was organisationally weak, it possessed few resources for political mobilisation, and few members were politically experienced. In short, it was not ready to mount a bid for state power. In August 1963, however, its hand was forced. Britain announced that a conference would be convened to discuss constitutional change in Fiji. The tide had turned and pointed in one direction. Independence was coming, whether Fijians wanted it or not. Their leaders realised this. State power was at stake and so too the economic benefits that flow from it. Preparations had to be made. The level of Fijian political activity now increased accordingly.

Branches of the Fijian Association were established around the country and at major meetings in June 1964 and January 1965 the Association considered its position on constitutional change. A critical issue was the electoral roll. The Indian–dominated Federation Party pressed for a common roll for all voters. Fijians and Europeans opposed a common roll, fearing that, with Indians being the majority, it would favour the Indian–dominated Federation Party. Racial tensions mounted.

But the Indian community was by no means united. Hindus and Muslims did not see eye-to-eye; both were split into sects and factions; Indians of northern Indian origin did not always get on with those of southern Indian origin. In the cane fields, Indian workers were exploited by large Indian farmers as well as by Indian businesses. In addition, Gujerati commercial success was a source of jealousy and resentment among many other Indians. And, very importantly, not all Indians supported the Federation Party.

Especially among Muslims, Indian businesses, and Indian professionals, there was a belief that their interests would not be well-served by an independent Fiji run by the Federation Party. The two major Indian cane farmer organisations were the Kisan Sangh and the Maha Sangh. The south Indian derived Maha Sangh was closely aligned with the Federation Party, but the older of the two, the north Indian–derived Kisan Sangh, was more closely linked with Indian businesses, and in January 1965 its secretary, Ayodhya Prasad, initiated the formation of a National Congress of Fiji as a rival to the Federation Party.

The Fijian leadership saw in these divisions very real possibilities for an alliance. In a strategic political move, the Fijian Association decided to hold joint discussions with anti-Federation Indians on the forthcoming constitutional conference scheduled for August 1965. Its goal was to consolidate support for separate communal rolls.

This calculated move marked the beginning of a major turnaround in the dynamics of race and class in Fiji. By building bridges with certain sections of the Indian community, the Fijian Association hoped to weaken support for a common electoral roll. But there was an even bigger advantage. Such an alliance would be multiracial. If the Fijian Association could bring together – and dominate – a multiracial grouping, its bargaining position would be considerably strengthened. In addition, being more 'representative' of Fiji society, it might also be more appealing and acceptable to Fiji's electors.

On 25 June 1965 a historic meeting took place in Suva between the National Congress and the Fijian Association leadership. Also attending were European political leaders. The meeting declared itself a 'turning point towards racial understanding and tolerance at a responsible level'. It reached unanimous decisions on a number of constitutional matters and declared that similar meetings would be held before and after the constitutional conference in London in order to 'maintain the goodwill created and to put into resolute action the decisions made . . .'[21] At one of those meetings in July, representatives of the Chinese and various Pacific Island communities gave their full support and agreed that they be represented at the forthcoming constitutional conference by the Fijian and European delegates.

The conference in London ended on 9 August 1965. Among its principal recommendations were an enlarged Legislative Council with 14 Fijians, 12 Indian and 10 General Elector seats; a ministerial system of government; and, very importantly, retention of separate communal electoral rolls. Eight months later, in February 1966, the General Electors Association (GEA) was formed. A few days later a meeting of 'more than 60 men and women of all of Fiji's major races' resolved to form a 'political alliance or organisation' concerned with the welfare of the people of Fiji. The following month the Alliance Party was formed. Dominated by the Fijian Association, its junior partners were the GEA and the Indian Alliance (which grew out of the National Congress of Fiji). Among its objectives was the promotion of 'goodwill, tolerance, understanding and harmony among all the Colony's communities'. Multiracialism was thus embraced as the central ideological platform of the party that would enjoy almost uninterrupted power in independent Fiji for 17 years.

This story is important because it shows not only that the struggle for Fijian political power was fought largely in the name of Fijian paramountcy, but also that this strategy contained the seeds of its own undoing. Multiracialism helped secure political power for the Fijian elite, but could it also secure the primary goal of Fijian paramountcy?

PARAMOUNTCY AND MULTIRACIALISM: FOIL AND FOLLY

Fijian paramountcy was an effective foil against the perceived Indian threat, but whether the political power it helped to secure would convert into real gains for all Fijians was another matter. The folly lay in believing that it would and, for the Alliance in particular, in assuming that the patently obvious contradictions between Fijian paramountcy and multiracialism could be contained.

Political power under the Alliance was certainly dominated by Fijians, but it was shared nonetheless, which meant that the party could not totally ignore the interests of its non-Fijian partners, including Indians. Did this mean that Indians were no longer the ogres they once were? Or was it more the case that some Indians were now all right?

These questions underline two key features about the battle for power: one, that it was essentially a struggle between competing elites; and two, that the ideology of multiracialism it gave birth to did not put an end to racialism. It is certainly true that ordinary people also participated in the struggle, but they were minor players. The elites – Fijian, European and Indian – called the shots and their positions were shaped by the realisation that for the victors, state power held out tantalising possibilities for enrichment. The Fijian elite emerged as the dominant victor and was not slow in exploiting those possibilities. But it was now caught up in a dilemma of its own making. How were they to pursue their interests without offending their political base? Multiracialism seemed a way out.

Before too long, however, ordinary Fijians sensed that something was not quite right. How precisely did this official ideology of 'their' political party sit with the notion of Fijian paramountcy? In the past their leaders had incited them with talk of Indian domination. Now Indians were their political allies and multiracialism the party line. Had the threat vanished? How could they be sure that, in practice, multiracialism would improve their educational performance, give them more jobs, increase their representation in the professional classes, and make them successful business entrepreneurs? They could not. The evidence soon mounted that the Fijian elite prospered at their expense. The Alliance certainly used state resources to help Fijians, but only some Fijians benefited. After independence this class face of the indigenous question became clearer.

Following a second constitutional conference in 1969, Fiji became independent on 10 October 1970. Ratu Sir Kamisese Mara, leader of the Alliance Party and former Chief Minister, became Fiji's first Prime Minister. At the outset his government announced its intention to adopt policies for Fijian advancement. Improved educational performance and greater Fijian involvement in business topped the agenda; not surprising, given that Fijian political power had been achieved and Fijian culture was very much alive. Among the proposals were these: 50 per cent of government scholarships for Fijians; preferential loans; establishment of a special institute to train Fijians in business practice; increasing the number of Fijian companies; reservation of certain lines of goods for sale exclusively by Fijians; and racial parity in the public service. Time would be needed for implementation, but to Fijians at least this sounded good and the Alliance won the 1972 election with a comfortable majority of 14 in the 52-seat House of Representatives.

But this outcome was also the result of a complex voting system. Electors held four votes: a 'communal' one for a candidate of the same race; and three 'national' votes across racial lines; that is, one each for a Fijian, an Indian and a General Elector candidate. It was this system of cross-voting that allowed the Alliance to secure non-Fijian electoral support.

The Alliance's victory was the high point of its honeymoon period. Its first real test was just around the corner. In the following year Sakeasi Butadroka, a Fijian and Assistant Minister for Commerce and Industry, launched a scathing attack on the Alliance Government and Prime Minister Mara for not doing enough for Fijians. A former cooperatives officer who had spent a great deal of time with grassroots Fijians, especially in rural areas, Butadroka's primary concern was Fijian economic development. For him two years of Alliance rule was more than enough time to produce results. But the government, a Fijian-dominated one at that, had failed to do it.

Butadroka was promptly dismissed from his post and the party, but he remained as an independent in Parliament, where he continued his attacks. In 1974 he formed the Fijian Nationalist Party (FNP). But Butadroka's declared enemies were not only Mara and his government but Indians as well. Indians were also blamed for 'Fijian economic backwardness' and the rabid nationalist's vehement anti-Indian outbursts found support among other discontented Fijians. Multiracialism was the official line, but racialism was still very much alive.

Stung into action, the Alliance Government pursued its affirmative action policies with renewed urgency. We will show later that these policies were flawed in various ways, but the Alliance's most fundamental mistake was its failure to distribute the benefits of these policies fairly among Fijians. On this Butadroka and his party, now firmly established as the spearhead of Fijian nationalism, had no doubt:

> The only Fijians who seem to be getting ahead are those who do not do any useful work, they are the Government Ministers. As the Fijian saying goes: *e votavota o Tuirara* [which means 'the village headman who usually divides the feast normally leaves the largest portion for himself'] . . . Fijians are far behind as regards owning those things which stand as symbols for social and economic development, eg, bus, house, car, telephone and industries. This is due to the weakness and blindness of the Alliance Government.[22]

What was the Alliance's 'weakness'? For the nationalists it meant, in part at least, the Alliance pandering to Indian interests. Nowhere was this more evident than its position on the highly sensitive matter of native land. Indian farmers were concerned about the security of their land leases and persistent pressure led in November 1976 to the Agricultural Landlords and Tenants Act (ALTA). Among other things, it set the minimum lease period for native land at 30 years and allowed for further extensions of 20 years. Compelled by its policy of multiracialism and its need for Indian electoral support, the Alliance could hardly have done otherwise. But for Butadroka and his supporters this was simply too much. They whipped up a frenzy of extremist nationalism such as had never been witnessed in Fiji before. By the time the next election came around in April 1977, the stage was set for the Alliance's downfall.

In addition to renewing Butadroka's call to send Indians back to India, his party's election manifesto foreshadowed with chilling accuracy many of the extremist demands implemented 10 years later by Rabuka's Republic:

The interests of Fijians will be paramount at all times.

The Fijians must always hold the positions of Governor General, Prime Minister, Minister for Fijian Affairs and Rural Development, Minister for Lands, Minister for Education, Minister for Agriculture, Minister for Home Affairs and Minister for Commerce, Industry and Co-operatives.

More opportunities should be given for Fijians to enter into business.

Strengthen Fijian Administration and the Government should give it financial backing and support.

Establish a Fijian Institute to teach Fijians business.

The return to Fijians of all land that was sold illegally.[23]

As if Fijian disaffection was not enough, the contradiction between Fijian paramountcy and multiracialism made matters worse for the Alliance. What gains it might reasonably have expected as a result of ALTA were negated by an education policy announced just one month before the election. Fijian education performance lagged behind that of other racial groups and the

Alliance sought to address this through an affirmative action program. It decided that to be eligible for a scholarship to undertake a pre-degree program at the University of the South Pacific, Indian students would need a minimum pass mark of 261 in the New Zealand University Entrance Examination, whereas Fijian students would need only 216 marks. The Indian community was outraged and swung its votes behind the (now National) Federation Party (NFP). With 26 seats, it won the election by an outright majority of two. The Alliance gained 22 seats. Butadroka and western independent, Ratu Osea Gavidi, won two other seats. Overall, Fijian support for the Alliance fell by nearly 19 per cent. Fijian disaffection, exploited effectively by extremist nationalists, was the cause.

Fear and apprehension gripped the country. How would Fijians react to an Indian government? Would the overwhelmingly Fijian military intervene? Indeed, Rabuka later alleged that a coup had been contemplated.[24] But it proved unnecessary. Divisions within the NFP meant that it could not move quickly and decisively to form government. The party even made overtures to the Alliance to form a government of national unity, but Mara would have none of it. Instead, Ratu Sir George Cakobau, the Governor General and *Vunivalu* of Bau, appointed Mara to head a caretaker government until fresh elections could be held. Stunned, the NFP denounced the move but could do nothing to stop it.

The details of the crisis that followed are less important here than its general effects: denial of the democratic process and a deepening of racial fear. Not surprisingly, then, in the subsequent elections of September 1977 Fijians flocked back to the Alliance. The Alliance focused its attack on the nationalists and, assisted by divisions within the NFP, won a massive majority of 21. But if ordinary Fijians thought that a return to Fijian political paramountcy would this time improve their lot, they were soon disappointed. That disappointment slashed the Alliance's majority in 1982 to a mere four seats.

The Alliance's cause was not helped by the recession of 1982 that saw the economy fall in real terms by 1.1 per cent. Now back in office with a slender majority, the Alliance's problems continued, a major one being its long-running dispute with the country's largest trade union, the Fiji Public Servants Association, over salaries and working conditions. The dispute, which began in early 1980, continued to dog the Government and eventually, in August 1984, a compromise was reached. But public servants, including Fijian ones, remained unhappy and three months later their anger boiled over.

With the economy again heading into recession, the Fijian Finance Minister delivered his budget for 1985. He announced retrenchments in the public service and a freeze on all wages, salaries and increments. The reaction from the labour movement was swift and strong. One month after the budget was announced the Fiji Trades Union Congress decided unanimously to form a Fiji Labour Party. In 1985 as the recession deepened, the economy registered a growth rate of −4.8 per cent. The situation was ripe for the Fiji Labour Party. Workers were angry and many were urban Fijians.

The Labour Party was officially launched in July 1985. It declared its commitment to end the politics of race and fear, and to work for all Fijians whatever their race. It was especially concerned to improve the lot of Fiji's disadvantaged. In his launching address, party president Dr Timoci Bavadra, a Fijian from the village of Viseisei on the outskirts of the western sugar city of Lautoka, described the FLP's origins.

As responsible trade unionists we felt compelled to react strongly to government policies that threaten the wellbeing of our members and, in fact, of all Fijians. We recognised that it was time for the working people of Fiji to form their own political party rather than continue to rely on the goodwill of existing political parties that increasingly had demonstrated that they represent only the narrowest interests ... What has become apparent to more and more people in Fiji is that a tremendous gap exists between the rhetoric by which the ruling party claims to be serving the interests of the people of Fiji and the reality. Whether one be a civil servant, cane farmer, copra cutter or urban labourer, it is obvious that the Government is not doing enough and that it has become increasingly distant from the majority of people ...

Our aim is to provide a real alternative to this rhetoric to create a political force that truly represents and is responsive to the needs, aspirations
and will of the people of Fiji. Our aim is the creation of true democracy
in this country and to put an end to the many undemocratic features that
dominate the political life of Fiji . . . I would like to reiterate the call of the
FLP to do something about the disadvantaged groups within our society
who have been neglected for far too long, and whose lives have become
marginalised.[25]

This message was not lost on ordinary Fijians. Indeed it appealed especially
to urban Fijians and they responded in the April 1987 election by delivering government to the Labour Party in coalition with the NFP. But the
victory was short-lived.

One month later, on 14 May, Bavadra's racially balanced government
was overthrown by a military coup led by Lieutenant Colonel Sitiveni
Rabuka. He plotted with the extremist Taukei Movement that represented
politicians and chiefs keen to restore the old order. It also represented a
rising group of business people and technocrats who deeply resented the
loss of patronage the change in government threatened. Rabuka justified
his coup in the name of defending Fijian interests.

But Rabuka was a commoner, and although the chiefs as a whole rapidly
endorsed his coup, they were shocked at the disrespect the Taukei Movement
and its leaders displayed towards them. This disrespect underlined growing
commoner rebelliousness, a major reason for chiefly attempts during the
1980s to reassert their authority by reinstating their long-defunct powers
under the old Fijian Administration. But it was too late. The commoner
genie was already out and Rabuka demonstrated just how powerless the
chiefs had become.

In September 1987, Mara and the Governor General, Ratu Penaia Ganilau
(another eastern high chief) decided that the only way to restore confidence
in Fiji's rapidly faltering economy was to reconcile the two major communities with a government of national unity. Rabuka retaliated with a second
coup and declared Fiji a republic. The high chiefs never fully recovered

from the blow. Although Ganilau returned as President at the end of 1987 and Mara once more became Prime Minister, it was under terms largely dictated by Rabuka. Indeed, Mara's next four years in office were shaped by conflict with the new interloper.

Rabuka's commoner status added to his appeal among Fijians. But he was also strongly connected with three important Fijian institutions – the army, the Methodist Church, and the elite Queen Victoria School. By 1990 he had got his way and a new Constitution instituted a system of apartheid which deliberately marginalised Indians. The electoral system heavily favoured Fijians, particularly eastern Fijians from the old chiefly strongholds in Tailevu, Lau and Cakaudrove. By contrast, western and urban Fijians were grossly under-represented. All senior political and bureaucratic positions were reserved for Fijians. But undoubtedly the worst affected by this system of apartheid were Indians.

In 1991 Rabuka defeated Mara's wife (a powerful chief in her own right) to head a new political party sponsored by the Great Council of Chiefs called the SVT (*Soqosoqo ni Vakavulewa ni Taukei*). In the 1992 election under his new Constitution, Rabuka succeeded Mara as Prime Minister, and the so-called Fijian revolution began. But what hopes the disadvantaged Fijian masses had that they would benefit from this revolution were soon dashed. As we will show in the next chapter, the main beneficiaries of Rabuka's agenda to address 'Fijian economic disadvantage' were the elites. Consequently ordinary Fijians became increasingly disaffected.

But Rabuka's woes were worsened by a sluggish economy in desperate need of investment, by local Indian businesses among others. Fiji faced serious difficulties. Services languished, poverty threatened nearly 60 per cent of the population, increasing numbers of children suffered from malnutrition, and continued rural neglect saw Suva's shanty-towns expand to include one in seven of the population. By 1995 unrestrained borrowing had become so extensive that the National Bank of Fiji collapsed.

These social and economic consequences of Rabuka's post-coup management, coupled with growing domestic and international pressure for a return to democracy, finally led Rabuka to extend an olive branch to the Indian communities. After wide consultations with Fiji's peoples, a new Constitution was adopted in 1997. Fresh elections were held in May 1999. Electors turned on Rabuka and directed their preferences to Labour, which had languished after 1994. The unexpected victory stunned Rabuka. It underlined his failure to resolve the indigenous question.

The 1997 Constitution was more democratic and less discriminatory than the 1990 Constitution. But it still divided Fiji's peoples into the racial compartments and conflicting interests that had failed the country in the past. Rabuka had used racial distinctions and the idea of Fijian paramountcy to justify both his coups and the separate economic strategies for different races he pursued afterwards. But these missed the point.

The Alliance Government lost office in April 1977 and May 1987 essentially because it did not address the concerns of ordinary Fijians. In 1977 it lost rural Fijian support and in 1987 the support of the growing urban Fijian community. Despite all their differences, Butadroka and Bavadra represented two sides of the same coin. They recognised that the Alliance's declining political legitimacy and electoral defeats were due primarily to its failure to rectify the disadvantage of ordinary Fijians. Post-coup governments did not recognise this. Consequently they repeated all the mistakes of the Alliance. And like the Alliance, when pressures to address Fijian disadvantage became irresistible, they chose to focus on the racial issue as if this would be enough to offset the contradictions inherent in their economic policies. A more democratic Constitution would appease Indians. It would generate greater Indian investment in the economy. A more vibrant economy would benefit everyone.

Not surprisingly, Fijian nationalists remained dissatisfied. Concessions to 'Fijian interests' in the 1997 Constitution did not address Fijian commoner disadvantage. As in 1987, the Labour Party specifically targeted this discrepancy and won a landslide victory in the 1999 election. And the losers, instead of absorbing the lesson, simply repeated the mistakes of their predecessors. They reached for the racial card and began a campaign of destabilisation once more. Why? The answers, we believe, lie both in the ideology of Fijian paramountcy and in the policies they had always adopted to address Fijian disadvantage. We take this up more fully in the next chapter.

TOWARDS 2000

What, then, are the major threads to be drawn from this brief historical discussion of the indigenous question?

First, the issue of indigenousness is not at all clear-cut. Who, exactly, is indigenous is contested. So too is the understanding of what precisely being indigenous means. Fijians are not, and never were, a homogenous and united people. It is not surprising, therefore, that there are disagreements, including among Fijians, about what precisely 'Fijian culture and tradition' consist of. There are certainly broad cultural similarities between the various Fijian communities but there are differences as well.

Second, at the core of indigenous concerns is a perception of threat from Indians. We have shown that this perception is unfounded, but we also acknowledge that its persistence has important political, economic and social effects. The challenge is to correct the misperception.

Third, indigenous strategies to address the perceived threat have been based on the notion of and call for Fijian paramountcy. From the history of the struggle for Fijian paramountcy, we learn that the main beneficiaries were not the vast majority of ordinary Fijians, but the Fijian elite.

Fourth, this elite bias was heightened by the introduction of multiracialism in the mid-1960s as a means to ensure the Fijian elite's political dominance in independent Fiji.

Fifth, apart from their elite bias, Fijian paramountcy and multiracialism were inherently contradictory. After independence the contradictions intensified. Those contradictions, along with elite bias, were the key underlying causes of the growing crisis of legitimacy of the Alliance between 1972 and 1987 and the coups of 1987. They also lay at the heart of Fijian nationalist opposition to a return to democracy. The 1990 Constitution was the highest political expression of extremist nationalist aspirations but, as the ensuing years revealed, it too did little to address the plight of ordinary Fijians. Their growing disaffection was an important reason for the partial return to democracy under the 1997 Constitution but the events of 2000 showed that the yearning for Fijian paramountcy was still strong.

So where to from here? Missing from our story is another strand that is so critical that it requires separate discussion. Its roots lie deep in Fiji's colonial history, and we will refer to that, but we will focus mainly on the period since 1987. Cutting across, and greatly complicating, the struggle for a return to democracy after 1987 was the other critical strand of the indigenous question, 'Fijian economic disadvantage'. Fijian supremacy meant little without 'Fijian economic power' and, as in the past, nationalists relied on the notion of Fijian paramountcy to justify affirmative action as the way to correct Fijian economic disadvantage and, beyond that, secure Fijian economic power. By the mid-1990s, however, the contradictions and elite biases of that strategy were increasingly revealed. To shore it up, Fijian nationalists gave a new twist to the indigenous question.

Fijian paramountcy still remained the ultimate goal, but in the face of growing discontent over its ugly, racist and anti-democratic character, the nationalist agenda was increasingly couched in terms of the need to protect indigenous rights. It was only a matter of time before this new twist would come to the fore in a much more open and assertive way. In 2000 it did. To that story we now turn.

Chapter 3

Disadvantage and indigenous rights: myths, realities, strategies

WE HAVE SHOWN THAT the long-standing Fijian perception of the 'threat of Indian domination' is unfounded. Fijians own most of the land and they still have their cultures and traditions. When the British left they assumed political control and, apart from a period of about 40 years, they have always dominated Fiji demographically. It is only in the economic area that they perceive themselves as still lagging behind other communities. In fact, it is their 'economic disadvantage' that is the least-resolved aspect of the indigenous question. Not that the related cultural, land, political and demographic aspects have been resolved. They have not. It is simply that, when all is said and done, without a sense of economic well-being, everything else is likely to remain a problem.

ECONOMIC DISADVANTAGE

Concern about 'Fijian economic disadvantage' goes back to the colonial period, but what exactly does it mean, and what is needed to resolve it? Put differently, what would Fijian economic success entail? Before addressing this question, one important matter needs to be cleared up.

Economic success is here understood in the capitalist sense. It is important to state this at the outset because a different case could be advanced
on the basis that economic success in the traditional Fijian sense means
something different, and Fijians might prefer that. The argument would be
based on the premise that Fijian cultures and traditions are based on non-
capitalist values. But the exact nature of economic success based on such
values needs to be spelled out. To our knowledge this has never been done,
certainly not by Fijian nationalists who, in the name of Fijian paramountcy,
insist on the preservation and protection of Fijian cultures and traditions.

Even if there were agreement on the meaning of Fijian economic success
in a traditional sense (and there is not), the key issue is that Fijians are
faced with a choice. Either, as has often been said, they cling to their cultures
and traditions and continue to lag behind others economically, or they adjust
and make compromises to better enable them to achieve greater economic
success in the capitalist sense. They cannot have it both ways, and most
people know this. It is patently obvious that the very ones who spearhead
the push for greater Fijian economic success – the Fijian elite – are very
clear about what economic success means, to them at least. And it is not
some obscure notion based on 'traditional Fijian culture'. This is also true
of Fijians generally. What, then, of economic success in the capitalist sense,
and where does it sit on the question of Fijian economic disadvantage?

First, income (cash) and wealth (assets) indicate economic success in the
capitalist sense. Fijians, like others, want both.

Second, economic success is absolute and relative. Absolute economic
success is where there is enough income and wealth to meet personal and
family needs and aspirations; relative economic success is where income
and wealth levels compare favourably with that of others. Both are important, but more so because of the highly charged political struggles around
Fijian paramountcy. What increasingly drives the political agenda is the
perception that other racial groups, especially the Indians, are economically
more successful than Fijians.

Third, economic success is more likely with high salaries or high profits.
Highly paid employment and business success are therefore the main routes

to economic success. The Fijian complaint is that neither route, particularly the second, has been especially open to them. Which is why they assert the need for economic affirmative action.

Fourth, economic success is more likely with, among other things, skills, qualifications, hard work, discipline, frugality, acumen and investment capital. The debate about this in relation to Fijians has been around for some time, and we will pick up on it later. But here we state the obvious point that capital can be accumulated through saving or borrowing. This point is important because in the Fijian case there is another method of accumulation that is not, strictly speaking, either saving or borrowing. *Soli vakavanua* is the traditional practice of collective giving and, as we will see later, is an important means for capital accumulation.

On the basis of this account, Fijian economic disadvantage would mean either (i) in the absolute sense, Fijians as a whole have insufficient income or assets to meet personal and family needs or (ii) in the comparative sense, their levels of income or assets are lower relative to others. But neither proposition is true. As we will show in this chapter, not all Fijians are economically disadvantaged in either sense. This is true even for rural Fijians. Villages conceal vast differences in wealth, with the top 20 per cent of village households in 1996 receiving seven times the income of the poorest 20 per cent. Poverty affects all communities, and unevenly.[1]

Furthermore, it is not necessarily true that economic disadvantage is greater in Fijian communities than others. Research conducted in the early 1990s found, for example, that 79 per cent of Fijians and 89 per cent of Indians belonged to disadvantaged classes – small farmers, wage workers, the peasantry, unpaid family workers and the unemployed.[2] Poverty reports later in the decade lend support to this finding. Slightly more Indians lived below the poverty line than Fijians; two-thirds of the poor in both communities were in rural areas.

Despite such evidence, Fijian perceptions of economic disadvantage as a racial phenomenon remain strong, the more so because they bring into sharp focus political tensions around economic affirmative action, the strategy employed by successive governments to address this problem. However,

Fijian economic disadvantage is not discussed in these terms. Instead discussion centres principally on the under-representation of Fijians in the professional classes and the poor record of Fijians in business. We focus on Fijian calls for affirmative action to address these two examples of disadvantage and the difficulties they have generated.

AFFIRMATIVE ACTION 1: EDUCATION AND THE PROFESSIONS

During the colonial period, the main route to Fijian economic advancement was through paid employment: labouring jobs; white-collar work in the colonial civil service (especially the Fijian Administration); and a few professional areas such as nursing, teaching, and later politics. But these options were open to only a small proportion of Fijians who managed to acquire formal qualifications or relevant experience, or who were well-connected.

As was the case during the colonial period, after independence the government remained the largest single employer. It was there that Fijian workers were most highly concentrated. But for a long time there were more Indians than Fijians in the mainstream bureaucracy, which is why the call went out for racial parity in the public service. The Fijian push for this grew stronger during the period of Fijian political leadership under Mara, and peaked after the coups of 1987. Between 1987 and 1989, for example, about 1,000 Indians left the public service and the number of new Fijian appointments was three times the figure for Indians.[3]

The Fijianisation of the public service was led by a group of disgruntled Fijian public servants who broke away from the Fiji Public Service Association to form the Viti Civil Service Association. Today the public service, including its highest levels, is dominated by Fijians. The same is true of most statutory authorities.

For these Fijians, privileged to have work and security of tenure, life is much easier than for the much larger number who have less well-paid jobs or do not have paid jobs at all. Their interest in ensuring the continuation of Fijian state power is therefore obvious – all the more so for the small elite at the top of the bureaucracy and the Fijian political masters they serve. But the story of Fijian economic advancement in the private sector is rather different.

We have already exposed the myth that Indians dominate the economy and are the cause of Fijian economic disadvantage. But the myth continues, and Fijian resentment is aimed not only at Indian businesses but also at Indian professionals. Fijians have long bemoaned Indian predominance in the professions, especially accountancy, economics, finance, insurance, law, engineering, medicine and, more recently, information technology. But Indian professional achievement was not handed to them on a platter. From their early days in Fiji, Indians – who had little else to fall back on – have always attached great importance to education. Through sacrifice and hard work, many succeeded.

By comparison, the record of Fijian educational achievement has not been as good. Between 1984 and 1999, for example, only 11 per cent of Fijian students reached the final year of high school, compared with 26 per cent of Indian students. Also, of the 6,252 Fijian students on tertiary scholarships, only 39 per cent graduated.[4] Communal demands have been cited as a reason for their relatively poor record. But this is a cultural matter that only Fijians can resolve. Either they maintain their culture and its various demands, in which case they should not complain, or they help their children by ensuring that cultural demands do not get in the way of their educational efforts.

Another reason cited is lack of resources. This is a long-standing and serious constraint that will not be removed until Fijians increase their incomes. But the state has also responded to this problem and, again, its response has been to apply the policy of affirmative action in the area of education. Successive governments put extra resources into Fijian education and there are now more Fijians in the professional classes. But they are still heavily concentrated in a few areas, notably teaching, medicine and the law. They have yet to make their mark in critical areas like commerce, finance, engineering and information technology.

There is also another downside, for the evidence suggests that Fijian professional advancement has benefited the Fijian elite more than ordinary Fijians. Nowhere is this more evident than in the allocation of government scholarships for tertiary studies. According to sociologist Vijay Naidu: 'There does not seem to be any application of a means test. Thus relatively well-off ethnic Fijians have access to these scholarships.' This is reminiscent of earlier days when some overseas awards, particularly to pursue law degrees, 'went to children of prominent ethnic Fijians although other Fijians with better aggregate scores were by passed'.[5]

Important though they are, cultural demands and resource constraints do not fully explain the comparatively poor record of Fijian educational achievement. Hard work is also necessary and, in the view of some teachers, a great deal more of it needs to be shown by Fijian students. Whether and how this is to be encouraged is, again, a matter for Fijians to decide. And decide they must. Formal qualifications do not come easily, and formal qualifications matter when it comes to membership of the professional classes. There is simply no substitute for hard work, and many Fijians know this. As one put it with ruthless and refreshing honesty, Fijian aspirations are nothing 'without Fijian perspiration'.[6]

AFFIRMATIVE ACTION 2: FIJIANS IN BUSINESS

Above all else, Fijians have seen business success as the hallmark of their economic advancement, and economic affirmative action the route to its achievement. Two questions arise here. The first concerns the capacity of the state to implement affirmative action. Essentially, it has been limited, and limited in three important ways.

First, the state did not have unlimited resources, and competition for them was great. Second, the power of non-Fijian business interests has been such that the state risked dire economic consequences if it seriously offended those interests in pursuing its affirmative action agenda. And it did not. Third, the state has not been immune to the forces of globalisation. It might for some time resist the international push for greater democracy and respect for human rights – and it did – but the imperative of trade liberalisation and economic reform was another matter. Affirmative action was an impediment to these changes and both internal and external pressures forced the state at various times to ease up on this policy.[7]

The second question is this: for which Fijians was business success a realistic goal? Put another way, who precisely benefited from economic affirmative action? Clearly not the vast majority of Fijians – subsistence farmers, low-paid workers, the unemployed and so on. For them, income to meet basic needs was the best they could hope for. They simply did not have the experience, capital and connections to make it in business. The same is true for the small but significant proportion of Fijians involved in tiny, informally-operated enterprises such as producing and selling produce and handcrafts in local markets, selling prepared food to wharf and factory workers, and grass-cutting. These are the Fijians who have languished at the bottom of the economic heap and continue to do so. For them economic affirmative action is little more than words. For a small minority, affirmative action did promise success, although in the end many of them failed and even those who survived cannot yet claim to represent a successful Fijian business class.

With Fijians commanding political power since independence, successive governments adopted the policy of economic affirmative action and deployed state resources to 'help Fijians in business'. But their efforts did not produce a successful Fijian business class comparable with the Indian business class or, more to the point, with large foreign corporations. Recent research shows that in the three decades to 1986 the number of Fijian businesses increased dramatically, but these were overwhelmingly small-scale businesses in the informal sector. And they survived without state subsidy. Far fewer Fijian businesses were in the formal and large-scale business sector. In June 1987, for example, only 15 per cent of Fiji's 700 registered companies were owned by Fijians[8].

What this suggests is that an established and competitive Fijian business class does not yet exist, but one is emerging. The Rabuka-led regime tried with greater vigour than the Alliance to hasten its development, and the interim Qarase regime made it a central feature of its Blueprint for Fijians. But it will be some time before this emergent class establishes itself as a significant, let alone dominant, player in the market. In this regard, however, we note the exceptional case of Fijian Holdings Limited (FHL) and will return to this later.

As well as for obvious economic reasons, the slow emergence of a Fijian business class is important politically. Increasingly, Fijians understand that Fijian paramountcy is meaningless without economic power. Despite its elite bias, therefore, a successful Fijian business class would at least convey the impression of Fijian economic advancement. This would make race relations less fraught and help calm political tensions. However, such a situation is unlikely to occur until the causes of Fijian tardiness are addressed. But first they need to be identified.

One explanation lies in the colonial system of Fijian administration. This system confined most Fijians to the subsistence economy and did not allow them to fully engage in the capitalist economy. It limited their roles to that of workers, small-time buyers and sellers, and landlords. But even where Fijians were landlords, bureaucracies like the Native Land Trust Board usurped their roles. This was the major complaint of Monasavu landowners in their claim for compensation for land around Fiji's hydro-electric power station. Bureaucratic development transferred few skills, it removed from them all responsibility and often all knowledge of development, and it denied them access to resources and involvement with their investments. Opportunities to get involved in business and acquire experience were therefore rare.

Fijian complaints about these historical legacies are entirely justified. So too are Fijian calls for assistance to overcome the economically debilitating effects of those legacies. But to lay blame at the feet of Indians, as some have done, is neither fair nor helpful. Nor, of course, is simply complaining about history without tackling the problem in the contemporary setting. In the end, the problem is here and now, and the here and now is rather different from colonial times.

Individual and cultural factors have also been identified as reasons for Fijian business failure. Alongside lack of application, hard work and sacrifice

on the part of individuals, various cultural aspects are often raised as imped-
iments to free enterprise, as well as restricting resources needed for investment
and growth. Two examples are usually cited: customary obligations and
kerekere, a form of borrowing that carries both an expectation to give and
an obligation to reciprocate in the future. Fijian business people complain a
great deal about the widely held perception among Fijians that simply having
a business means that one is both wealthy and a legitimate target for *kerekere*.

But the fact that some Fijians have succeeded in business contradicts the
often-held stereotype that Fijians are incapable of business success. Many
people, including Fijians, acknowledge individual and cultural factors as
obstacles to Fijian business success. But only Fijians can address such obstacles. For example, one cause of failure is lack of capital, and Fijians might
do well to critically examine the way the practice of *soli vakavanua* has been
used as a means of raising capital.

The concept of *vanua* is central to the Fijian way of life and Fijian sociologist Steven Ratuva gives the most incisive account of how *soli vakavanua*
has been exploited by the Fijian elite for its benefit and to the detriment
of ordinary Fijians.

> *Vanua* refers to the relationship between the land and the people indige-
> nous to the land. Critically, this relationship is symbolised by chiefly power:
> the chief 'owns' the land and 'owns' the people. The relationship has both
> political and spiritual dimensions, and is thus intensely ideological. It can
> [also] have a material impact ... investable resources [can be raised by
> appealing to the] communal sense of obligation to the *vanua* ... [It is this
> kind of appeal that] inspires the altruism shown in *soli vakavanua*, or commu-
> nity collection: money is mobilised through neo-traditional festivals in which
> various tribal units compete. Indeed, tribal competition becomes an end in
> itself because winning, and the publicity generated by winning, becomes a
> source of pride for the *vanua*. As a result, provinces are continually engaged
> in competition over their *soli vakavanua*.
>
> [For] members of the *vanua*, however, competition [in the *soli vakavanua*]
> is a rivalry over the accumulation of <u>social</u> assets (emphasis added) such as

prestige, rather than the [accumulation] of capital for investment in the market. Similarly, ownership of a company that [results] from *soli vakavanua* is not seen as a means towards accumulation but as an expression of political prestige for the *vanua* and its symbolic representation, the chief. Indeed, there is a painful psychological sanction [for] failure to mobilise resources: it is an insult to the *vanua*, the chief and to ethnic Fijians themselves.[9]

In the 1970s the establishment of provincial council companies marked a new effort to increase Fijian business activity. Heralded as a major step in Fijian economic advancement, these companies used money raised through *soli vakavanua* to fund their investments. As Ratuva explains: 'In the various investments made by the Provincial Councils, chiefs were often made the legal holders of shares, the legal holders of company titles, and the directors of any companies that were created.' What essentially happened was that 'primordial servitude [was] adapted to modern commercial capitalism'. This he calls 'communal capitalism'.[10]

But this, Ratuva argues, would not be exceptionable were it not 'exploitative in the sense that revenues generated were not distributed equitably'. As he put it, there was very little 'trickle down' to ordinary Fijians. In the case of provincial council companies, 'A substantial amount of the surplus was used to finance the administrative operation of the Provincial Councils; it thus served to sustain an ethnic Fijian bureaucratic strata. It was not distributed as dividends to individual ethnic Fijians, which would be the normal practice, and which might have assisted in the alleviation of rural poverty.'[11]

Moreover, many of the provincial council companies formed partnerships, 'based on political cronyism and economic expediency, with foreign companies with interests in logging, hotels and other resource-based sectors'. In this way, 'some chiefs were able to acquire considerable personal benefit through the accumulation of wealth, while foreign and local non-ethnic Fijian companies benefited through political security and ready access to natural resources'. For ordinary Fijians, the tragedy was that personal and family savings that could have been used for daily sustenance and local investment were controlled by dominant and chiefly elites to sustain an agenda which had the appearance of enhancing Fijian economic development but in reality fulfilled the economic aspirations of elite Fijians.[12]

By the early 1980s the failure of communal capitalism to benefit the majority of Fijians became glaringly obvious. Their growing discontent worried the Fijian elite. In 1982 their political arm, the Alliance Government, had its parliamentary majority slashed from 14 to four. The task of developing a successful Fijian business class, which would at least meet the political goal of creating the impression of Fijian economic success, had failed. A new push was necessary.

In 1984, with Fijian disaffection on the rise, the overall strategy, economic affirmative action, and a particular one, communal capitalism, were brought together in an initiative that has since become the largest and single most important Fijian intervention in the corporate sector. In 1984 Fijian Holdings Limited, the 'flagship of Fijian communal investment', was formed. The story of its development further reveals the myth of Fijian economic disadvantage as well as exposing even more the elite bias of economic affirmative action as the overall strategy to redress that disadvantage.

A creation of the Great Council of Chiefs, FHL was mandated 'to increase Fijian participation in the commercial economy ... through acquisition in established, well-managed, profitable companies with excellent prospects for growth ... [and to ensure that the] benefits spread as widely as possible among the Fijian people'.[13] The goals were admirable, but in practice were not realised in large part because of the company's corporate culture and conflicts of interest.

Together, the Native Land Trust Board (NLTB) and the Fijian Affairs Board (FAB) hold about 27 per cent of FHL shares; private companies and small *tikina* (district) and *mataqali* groups hold the rest. We consider these in turn.

Ratuva argues that as an investor and guardian of Fijian land, the NLTB's record has been less than impressive. Rocked over the years by financial scandal, charges of nepotism, cronyism, corruption and sustained losses since 1986, the NLTB was on the verge of bankruptcy by 1997. Many questions have been raised about this sorry state of affairs, including by Fijians like Ratuva who, citing specific examples, argues that the NLTB's difficulties are in part due to the extremely complex relationship between the state and chiefs in financial affairs, which in turn is symptomatic of a corporate culture that makes it difficult to distinguish between market, communal and personal interests.

On this basis he questions the NLTB's capacity for sound financial management and investment decisions and, more particularly, its investment in FHL as an economic affirmative action on behalf of Fijians. Despite official claims to the contrary, he says the organisation does not represent a homogenous Fijian interest but 'narrow parastatal, bureaucratic and private institutional interests, propagated as universally ethnic Fijian'. The NLTB's shares in the FHL therefore represent 'an entrepreneurial engagement that advances this narrow interest'.[14]

Outside of the NLTB, Fijian communal shareholding in FHL was funded by two other means: by money raised communally in the provinces and by taxpayers' money diverted by the state to the Fijian Affairs Board to purchase FHL shares for the purposes of economic affirmative action.

In relation to the first of these, we have already described how communal mobilisation of resources through *soli vakavanua* exploits ordinary Fijians and benefits the elite. Ratuva's research confirms this in relation to provincial investments in FHL shares. For ordinary Fijians, their stake in the FHL and the benefits they derived from it are minimal. On a per capita basis, their stake is tiny, not only in absolute terms but also in comparison to their individual contributions to communal collections that 'are often larger by a factor of 10'. Because of this, and the meagre dividends they receive, Ratuva argues, 'individual ethnic Fijians would have been better off keeping their donations to communal collections and investing it themselves'.[15]

As for the FAB, its initial shareholding in FHL was 100,000 A-class shares. Five years later, in 1989, this investment increased dramatically. In the previous year, the Rabuka regime, in its push to secure greater Fijian economic control, adopted a 'Nine Point Plan' drawn up by a group of Fijian intellectuals, professionals and bureaucrats who came together under an umbrella body called the Fijian Initiative Group. One of its key recommendations was that the FAB inject F$20 million into the FHL. The Government duly obliged and provided that sum in the form of an interest-free loan. With it the FAB bought 20 million B-class shares, each worth one dollar.

The main beneficiaries of dividends received by the FAB, Ratuva argues, are not ordinary Fijians but the FAB itself and the major interests it serves.[16] Owners of A-class shares also benefited, of course. They too received dividends generated by increased FHL activities that cost them nothing. Significantly, several members of Laisenia Qarase's Government, including Qarase himself, were shareholders or directors of FHL, sometimes both.[17]

The $20 million loan, the largest single amount disbursed under the banner of economic affirmative action, and recently converted to a grant by the Qarase regime, paved the way for a huge expansion. Paid-up capital increased dramatically and more interests were acquired in major companies in Fiji. By June 1999, operating revenue had grown to $45 million, operating profit after tax increased sevenfold to $7 million, total assets swelled from $1.3 million to $143 million, net assets surged from a mere $170,248 to over $73 million. Cash reserves stood at more than $9 million.[18] In the 1999/2000 financial year, after-tax profit reached $10.3 million.[19] Spectacular success, without doubt, and the company is poised to expand further, including internationally, according to management plans.

In part because of FHL's success, one writer has recently challenged the 'so-called weakness of ethnic Fijian business'. Scott MacWilliam, a political scientist at the University of the South Pacific, argues that a 'layer' of Indian and Fijian businesses has emerged in Fiji and that within that layer 'an ethnic Fijian bloc' has 'risen to the dominant position'. This case needs to be taken seriously. Unfortunately, MacWilliam does not provide details, although he is correct in saying that there are Fijian businesses in many, if not all, economic sectors. But in the context of the overall economy, just how significant are they? Does the existence of a few successful Fijian businesses, like FHL, mean that we can now talk of a successful Fijian business class?

This is arguable and, in any case, largely academic if, as MacWilliam himself acknowledges, the rise of Fijian businesses does not 'bring development'.[20] The more important point, which he does not make, is that from the viewpoint of race relations and political harmony, the rise of Fijian business must bring benefits to ordinary Fijians. The central point about economic affirmative action to help Fijians in business is that it is sustained by Fijian hopes that it will benefit them all. The overwhelming evidence is that it benefits only a minority. Understandably, anger among ordinary Fijians, which previously was targeted largely at Indian businesses, is now also aimed at Fijians ones, FHL included.

In 1992 FHL changed its status from a public limited company to a private limited company. The idea was to encourage more individual and group investors to invest in managed funds through FHL. This would kill two birds with one stone: first, it would allow FHL to expand its investment portfolio; and second, it would allow more individual and group investment by Fijians. Individual and group investments were limited to a maximum of $10,000 to ensure, in the company's words, that the 'benefits of Fijian Holdings shareholdings are spread as widely as possible'. And to ensure that only Fijians could buy into the managed funds, potential investors were limited to people listed in the *Vola ni Kawa Bula*, the Fijian Register. The problem, however, was that only a small proportion of Fijians had or could raise the money to invest. Even sums considerably less than the limit of $10,000 were beyond the reach of most.

Although intended and presented as a vehicle for economic advancement for Fijians as individuals, this economic affirmative scheme was never likely to benefit Fijians other than members of the elite. And it is the latter, Ratuva suggests, who predominate in the 'private companies and small groups' that account for the 73 per cent of FHL shares that the NLTB and FAB do not own. Most of these private companies 'are owned by individuals or groups of individuals who are established business people, professionals or bureaucrats' and this, coupled with the ethnic restriction on FHL share ownership, means that most of the shares are owned by the Fijian elite.[21] So much for helping the Fijian 'people', which is why questions need to be asked about FHL as a model for indigenous advancement.

FHL is essentially an investment company. It simply invests in other companies that promise a high return. This is a perfectly sensible capitalist activity. But whether it is an effective strategy for the advancement of Fijians as whole, especially the disadvantaged majority, is another matter. The story we have told raises doubts about FHL as a model for introducing Fijians to commerce, fostering greater grassroots entrepreneurship, and overcoming constraints to greater Fijian participation in a wider range of economic sectors. These are important questions because FHL appears, to the Fijian elite at least, to point to a better way for Fijian economic success than another institutional spearhead of economic affirmative action, the Fiji Development Bank (FDB).

From its early days the Alliance Government professed a commitment to helping rural Fijians and complained continually about the commercial banks' bias against agricultural lending. It is reasonable to expect, there-fore, that agriculture would figure prominently in the Government's lending policy, especially as its lending capacity was tiny compared to that of the commercial banks. It did, but not for long, because in the mid-1970s the Alliance decided to act on the long-standing view that Fijians ought get more involved in commerce and industry. Affirmative action, it also decided, was necessary to achieve this.

Among other things, a program of soft, preferential loans by the govern-ment-owned FDB to Fijians was introduced in 1975. Known as the Commercial Loans to Fijians Scheme, this program soon led to a decline in FDB agricultural loans. By 1985 they accounted for only 25 per cent of total funds lent. But even with the bulk of FDB funds going to commer-cial and industrial loans, Fijian success in those sectors was not guaranteed.

First, Fijians got most of the loans, but others got most of the money. In 1978, for example, Fijians got 71 per cent of the loans but only 28 per cent of the total value of loans. In 1985, the figures were 52 per cent and 8 per cent respectively.[22] The bank's public documents do not say if other borrowers include Indians or, if they do, in what proportions.

Second, and related to this, Fijians got much smaller loans than non-Fijians. In 1978, for example, non-Fijian loan amounts were three times that of Fijian ones. By 1985 they were 11 times as much.[23]

Third, large proportions of loans were in areas where the existing competition was well established, especially in transportation during the 1970s and 1980s and the retail sector in the 1990s.[24]

Fourth, a great deal of money went into real estate. The trend surged in the 1990s, peaking in 1995 when 62 per cent of loans were for real estate. In 1996, the figure fell only marginally to 58 per cent.

Fifth, the sector in which Fijians hoped so much to succeed fared the worst. Tourism loans generally accounted for less than 4 per cent of the total. In 1996, the figure was 0.5 per cent.

Sixth, and perhaps the most worrying trend of all, loans for investment in the productive sectors – manufacturing, construction and timber/agro-industry – were comparatively low. Hovering around 15 per cent of the total, they dipped in the 1990s and in 1996 stood at a miserable 0.7 per cent.[25]

Last, failure to meet loan repayments was common, so common in fact that a number of loan portfolios, including transport and real estate, were suspended. By 1996 total loan arrears stood at about $70 million.[26] In that year FDB profits fell by 83 per cent.[27]

What all this suggests is that the FDB certainly helped a lot of Fijians to get into business, but weaknesses in its lending policies and practices are partly responsible for the failure of a more substantial Fijian business class to emerge. It is one thing that the bank gave a large number of loans. Whether it lent wisely, however, is quite another matter and, on the evidence of past performance, key questions need to be asked.

In making so many small loans, did the bank seriously think that Fijian borrowers could realistically compete with larger competitors? Why did it so readily agree to loans in sectors where there were already established players, especially when they were unlikely to surrender their advantages easily? How, precisely, did it assess loan applications? Did it adequately take into account market conditions, or take them into account at all? Were assessors even aware of market conditions? Did the bank always heed market signals when Fijian businesses began to fail?

Only the bank can answer these questions, but Ratuva points to what the answer might be. Driven by the clamour for affirmative action, the bank responded to a political imperative without, it would appear, adhering strictly to the normal requirements of banking prudence. What mattered most was that the bank be seen to advance the affirmative action agenda. For this purpose, yardsticks were applied that were useful in a political sense but inadequate commercially. In the early years, much play was made of the large numbers of Fijians who received FDB loans. Later, during the early 1990s, the emphasis shifted to the size of loans but 'as in the past, the rate of return on investment was not a critical variable in judging success'.[28]

The other key financial institution under the economic affirmation action program, the National Bank of Fiji (NBF), was not spectacularly successful either. Early in 1995 its then head, the Rotuman Visanti Makrava, declared: 'I have done a lot to achieve the goals of the coups for Fijians and Rotumans.'[29]

The other side of this story is the collapse of the NBF. In November 1995 an audit of the bank revealed that it had been insolvent for four years. It had never made a profit. Since the 1987 coups, bad debts totalling $220 million, or 9 per cent of GDP, had been accrued because of the bank's failure to pursue established banking procedures. One individual obtained $637,790 on the strength of an uninsured truck valued at $15,000. Together with interest, the bad debts cost the Fiji public more than $330 million. Makrava was reluctant to say very much after these revelations: 'If I open my mouth, half the government goes, including the leader [Rabuka].'[30]

The NBF debacle was certainly a worry for the government, but behind it lay the bigger concern that economic affirmative action had not delivered on the economic aspirations of most ordinary Fijians. Despite this concern, no fundamental questioning of past strategies resulted. The old recipes, which benefited elites, continued, while the economic disadvantage of the vast majority of ordinary Fijians remained neglected. As we noted in Chapter 1, the interim administration in 2000 came up with yet another blueprint to address disadvantage. Is it any different from earlier ones, and is it likely to succeed? We suggest not.

FOR THE FUTURE: A BLUEPRINT OF FAILED RECIPES

Interim Prime Minister Qarase presented his Blueprint for Fijian Development[31] to the Great Council of Chiefs in July 2000. He said that 'much of the measures proposed' could be implemented in the next two years, but he also proposed that a 10-year plan for Fijian development be prepared.

The Blueprint contains new proposals; for example, royalty payments to landowners for mining and underground water. But it is unlikely that the additional income this would generate for individual landowners will be large, certainly not large enough to correct the economic disadvantage of most ordinary Fijians. Nor given the distribution formula applied by the Native Land Trust Board are they likely to reach the people who most need them.

Apart from such proposals, the Blueprint is essentially a repacking of old recipes, although this time with more assistance proposed. Its flavour is best captured by its own summary list, to which we add emphasis.

1. Government to provide a *grant* to establish a Fijian Development Trust Fund for investment to generate interest income to be used for, among other things: funding for the Fijian Foundation; leadership and other training programs; any other purposes approved by the Great Council of Chiefs (*including the financing of its own operations*).

2. A compulsory national savings scheme for Fijians to finance increased Fijian equity and other forms of participation in business, and also investment in education.

3. Government to recommence financial assistance to the NLTB through *annual grant support*.

4. Government to provide a **grant** to endow the proposed Fijian Development Trust Fund.

5. Government to provide **extra funding** to the Fijian Education Fund for more Fijian scholarships, more support for Fijian schools and research into Fijian educational issues.

6. Government to convert into a **grant** its $20 million interest-free loan to the Fijian Affairs Board to purchase shares in Fijian Holdings Limited. [This has been done.]

7. Government to provide an **interest-free loan to** Yasana Holdings Limited [**another Fijian company** similar to Fijian Holdings Limited].

8. **Reserve 50 per cent of Government shares** in companies **for Fijians** as they become available for sale to the public.

9. **Reserve 50 per cent of major licences for Fijians** (eg, import licences, taxi permits etc).

10. **Reserve 50 per cent of Government contracts for Fijians**.

11. **Continuation of the Fijian Development Bank (FDB) Loan Scheme** for Fijians but exclude other communities who are to be covered by a separate scheme at the FDB.

12. Reinstate Government budget provision of $500,000 to assist Fijians through interest-free loans to buy back ancestral land alienated as freehold land.

13. Government to reinstate **annual allocations of $1.5 million as grants, not interest-free loans, to Provincial Councils** for their participation in business.

14. Assistance to Fijian landowners who take up sugarcane farming on their reverted land.

15. Government to resume renting, on a needs basis, of commercial office buildings owned by Provincial and District companies.

16. Tax exemption for Fijian-owned companies for specified periods similar to existing tax concession schemes for particular sectors.

We make two points about this Blueprint. First, on the evidence of past performance, there is little reason to expect that this Blueprint is any more likely to redress the economic disadvantage of the majority of ordinary Fijians.

Second, it relies very heavily on government funding, much of it in the form of grants. But government money comes from taxpayers. And a great deal of that, if not the bulk, is paid by non-Fijian taxpayers. In the interests of helping disadvantaged Fijians and ensuring political stability, they may not mind this, but the question that needs to be asked is this: if implemented, how is it to be demonstrated that the Blueprint actually helps disadvantaged Fijians? The Blueprint is silent on this central issue.

Clearly some Fijians will benefit from the Blueprint, but which ones? More specifically, compared with the Fijian elite, what proportion of ordinary disadvantaged Fijians will benefit? This is the litmus test of success. But the Blueprint says nothing about this. There are no targets, no benchmarks, no performance indicators or measures. In short, there is no basis on which to assess outcomes.

As with previous blueprints, Qarase's initiative relies on taxpayers' money. The Government therefore owes it to taxpayers to show that their money is well spent, and well spent means that it is specifically targeted at economically disadvantaged Fijians rather than elite Fijians. The government needs to demonstrate this. To put it bluntly, taxpayers have a right to know what the return is on this investment of their money. Principles of accountability and transparency demand it. Stability demands it. If the events of 2000 are any indication, so do many disadvantaged Fijians.

GLOBALISATION AND THE LIMITS OF AFFIRMATIVE ACTION

In this discussion we have focused largely on local reasons for the failure of economic affirmative action to address the economic disadvantage of non-elite Fijians. But there were important external ones as well, and they became increasingly evident after the coups of 1987.

The severe economic downturn that followed the 1987 coups prompted the need for urgent remedial action. The post-coup regime could have responded in various ways. For example, it could have adopted inward-looking, protectionist policies. But it did not. Fiji was not immune to the global push for economic liberalisation and faced strong external pressure to go down that path.[32] It did. The post-coup state soon embarked on a major program of economic reform. It also believed that economic affirmative action could be pursued within that program. But the contradictions between economic liberalisation and affirmative action soon surfaced.

The showpiece of the economic reform agenda that followed the 1987 coups was the spectacular growth of the manufacturing sector. Central to this was the establishment of tax-free factories, most especially for garment production for export. Underpinning this shift towards export-oriented industrialisation was the policy of deregulation and the provision of highly attractive tax and other concessions. But international competitiveness required more than this. Labour market reforms began with the promulgation of draconian anti-labour legislation in 1991. A value-added tax was introduced in 1992 and further tax reforms came later. So too did financial sector reforms and public sector reforms, including downsizing, administrative reorganisation and performance-based remuneration. State enterprises were corporatised or privatised. What did this mean for the affirmative action agenda?

For ordinary Fijians it meant greater pain. Labour market reforms hurt them as workers. The value-added tax did not discriminate between ethnic groups. The pain of public sector reform fell increasingly on Fijian employees the more the public service was Fijianised. And the sale of state assets hurt the many Fijians employed in state-owned enterprises. In the face of such negative impacts, the significant level of Fijian support for wider worker struggles is not surprising. For the Fijian-dominated state this was a major concern, just as in the 1980s the very political support on which it depended most was being eroded.

Worried by this, the government began to waiver in its commitment to economic reform. By the mid-1990s its resolve was increasingly tested as competing interests in the private sector urged it in different directions. Fijian nationalists complained increasingly that the government was not doing enough to help Fijians in business. Yet again they raised the ogre of

'Indian' economic power and regularly reminded the government that its economic reforms undermined the policy of economic affirmative action. In the lead-up to the 1995 National Economic Summit, for example, the Summit Subcommittee on Indigenous Fijian Participation in Business again bemoaned the lack of Fijian business success and argued that the state had to soften its policy of deregulation.

> The government's deregulation policy runs contrary to its policy of enhancing indigenous Fijian business participation because most Fijians are involved in small enterprises which are in their infancy and cannot compete in terms of economies of scale and product quality with more established (and mostly Indian) companies which developed during Fiji's import-substitution era. Therefore, Fijian entrepreneurs should be protected ... Because of the need to replace market entry barriers for Fijians, they should get equal opportunities in government services that will be contracted out [as well as in] government entities to be privatised. Apart from a 50 per cent opportunity [for] Fijian business participation in the economy ... tenders by Fijian suppliers should enjoy a 15 per cent preference margin.[33]

Support for this view came from Finance Minister Berenado Vunibobo. Widely perceived as a hard-headed economic rationalist, he was also a nationalist and had no doubt about where the major threat to the nationalist agenda lay. For him the business community 'essentially belong[ed] to the Indian community' and affirmative action was necessary.

> The Fijians seem to have developed the feeling that by having political power, they are the master of the house. It doesn't work that way. You have to have a significant say in influencing the economy ... but at the end of the day the Indian business community could squeeze the country dry if they chose to do so because of their hold on the economic levers. The Fijians realise that now. That is why there is so much input, so much concern, about helping and encouraging Fijians to get into the economic mainstream.[34]

But the tide was already turning against the nationalist agenda and in the following year this became clearer. In August 1996 the Minister for Trade,

Industry, Commerce and Public Utilities, Isimeli Bose, announced a qualified softening of the deregulation policy. Competition would continue to be encouraged, but there would also be limits because, in his view, certain interests were much too important and had to be protected. Which interests? Certainly not Fijian ones, as the following report on an interview with the minister shows.

> He is keen on protecting the interests of local entrepreneurs – the Hari Punjas, the Vinod Patels and Mahendra Patels [all Gujeratis] – and long-established businesses such as Shell, Carlton Brewery and Morris Hedstrom [all foreign companies]. 'They have put their money where their mouth is.' Already the minister has advised the [Fiji Trade and Investment Board] to take special care of these local investors and make sure that they receive support ... And he is going to 'fight very hard' to protect the big local investors. 'I will run to their help whenever they need me.' While the minister is aware of the World Trade Organisation rules promoting a freer trading environment, Bose insists that at the end of the day, it's the national interest that 'must come first'.[35]

While the poor record of Fijian businesses continued to receive media attention, the government moved with renewed vigour at the end of 1996 to implement economic reforms. With the consequent shift from the nationalist agenda to a national one, only the most robust of Fijian businesses were likely to survive. The performance of companies like Fiji Holdings Ltd suggests that a Fijian business class, when it eventually emerges as a significant player in the market, will be dominated by a few large Fijian businesses controlled by elite Fijians.

What, then, does all this suggest about Fijian economic disadvantage and economic affirmative action as the strategy to address it?

First, economic disadvantage is not confined to Fijians. Second, not all Fijians are economically disadvantaged. Most are, some are not. This reveals the class face of the Fijian economic condition. Third, Indians do not dominate the economy, never have and are unlikely to do so. And they are not the cause of Fijian economic disadvantage.

Fourth, economic affirmative action has brought some improvement, but the Fijian elite has benefited much more than the majority of ordinary Fijians. Fifth, the problem with economic affirmative action as an attempt to address Fijian economic disadvantage is that it is not, as Ratuva put it, 'complemented with a program of poverty alleviation ... [an] alternative development paradigm suitable to the socio-economic conditions and limited resources of the majority of ethnic Fijians, especially the economically marginalised'.[36]

Sixth, by itself, affirmative action is not sufficient for Fijian economic advancement. Personal effort and commitment are also necessary, and perhaps cultural changes as well. Seventh, biases and deficiencies in key Fijian institutions need to be addressed.

Finally, there are serious constraints on the state's ability to resolve Fijian economic disadvantage. Apart from its limited resources, strong internal and external pressures for greater economic liberalisation have led to policies that hurt most ordinary Fijians. This suggests a need for government to use whatever leverage it has to get key actors in the private sector, foreign governments and international organisations to modify their policies and actions in a way that would help in the highly delicate task of alleviating the plight of ordinary Fijians without offending the rights and interests of other disadvantaged groups.

INDIGENOUS RIGHTS: THE NEW TWIST

We have already mentioned that local and external critics constantly reminded Fiji that economic affirmative action was an obstacle to open competition. It was one thing for government to help a particular group, quite another to discriminate against others in the process. But alongside global pressure for economic liberalisation, there was an international push for greater democratisation, and democratic forces in Fiji found international support for their struggle.

Initially, nationalists pressed on regardless and promulgated the 1990 Constitution. Over the next few years, however, divisions among Fijians deepened. This, coupled with continuing local and international pressure, tilted the balance against the nationalists. In 1992 the Fiji Labour Party supported the newly elected Prime Minister, Rabuka, in exchange for a review of the 1990 Constitution. The Rabuka regime prevaricated. Faced with growing Fijian disaffection resulting from an economic recession largely of its making, it needed to heed nationalist demands. But it also faced mounting local and international pressure not only for economic liberalisation but for a return to democracy as well. Eventually it yielded to that pressure and in July 1995 the review of the 1990 Constitution began.

The world watched very closely, and so too the majority of Fiji citizens, weary of economic hardship and political uncertainty. For their part, the nationalists could no longer count on the hard extremist line they previously followed. Something different was needed; something less offensive and hopefully more palatable and defensible. They saw possibilities in indigenous rights and drew on international efforts around the United Nations 'Draft Declaration on the Rights of Indigenous Peoples'. In the mistaken belief that the Draft Declaration promoted it, the Fijian party, the Soqosoqo ni Vakavulewa ni Taukei (SVT), told the Constitutional Review Commission (CRC) in October 1995 that political control 'is the collective right of self-determination of the indigenous people'.[37] This was, of course, challenged in other submissions. But the point is that a new twist was introduced into the debate and many Fijians, often uninformed, accepted it uncritically. In time the notion of indigenous rights gained wider currency in nationalist ranks and in 2000 emerged as the central focus of the debate. George Speight set the ball rolling when he declared that his coup had been staged to protect indigenous rights. But even if we assume that people know just what indigenous rights mean and where they sit in relation to other rights (and we cannot), is it the case that indigenous rights in Fiji were threatened? The answer to this question, basically, is no.

Fiji's constitutions (1970, 1990 and 1997) speak largely in terms of interests rather than rights. They all acknowledge the special interests of the Fijian people and contain provisions for their 'protection', 'preservation' and 'advancement'. Other communities are required to 'respect' these interests as well as Fijian aspirations. The ultimate constitutional protection has always been that any changes likely to affect Fijian interests, including land, required the agreement of huge majorities in both the House of Representatives and the Senate as well as the Great Council of Chiefs.

What greater guarantee of protection can there be? There is dictatorship, of course, and indeed many believed that Fiji leaned towards that under the 1990 Constitution, which opposition forces described as 'authoritarian, undemocratic, militaristic, racist and feudalistic'.[38] It provided for a 70-seat House of Representatives consisting of 37 Fijian, 27 Indian, five General Elector and one Rotuman seats. Among other things it established an electoral system that was heavily biased in favour of Fijians, strengthened the power of the Great Council of Chiefs, and restricted key positions to Fijians, including those of President, Prime Minister, Military Commander, Police Commissioner, Chief Justice, Head of the Public Service and Director of Public Prosecutions. Of course, there was no possibility that the NLTB, Fijian Affairs Board and Ministry of Fijian Affairs would be run by people other than Fijians.

Here, then, was a Constitution that was biased heavily in favour of Fijians. But any anticipation that it might help to unite Fijians was always unrealistic. Indeed, it had the opposite effect because its electoral provisions favoured some Fijians over others: rural Fijians (then 60 per cent of the Fijian population) received 30 seats, urban Fijians (40 per cent) seven seats. In addition eastern rural strongholds like Lau were privileged compared to more populous provinces like Ba in western Viti Levu.[39] During the 1990s the tensions generated by these constitutional arrangements encouraged further dissatisfaction among Fijians.

The 1997 Constitution was nowhere near as offensive as the 1990 one. It redressed the imbalances between Fijian provincial representation and provided urban Fijians with stronger representation. It also restored equity to Indian representation. Fijians received 23 communal seats, Indians nineteen. The new Constitution also provided for the protection of Fijian interests and, in so doing, also protected indigenous rights, as many people pointed out in the wake of May 2000 coup. Thus the ousted People's Coalition

Government was not alone in arguing – in its submission to the Africa-Caribbean-Pacific Fact-Finding Mission on the Fiji Crisis – that:

> The Fiji Islands Constitution is consistent and indeed it requires conformity with the International Convention on Civil and Political Rights, the Charter of the United Nations, the UN [Draft] Declaration on the Rights of Indigenous Peoples and other international standards.

A key objective of the Constitution is its commitment to protecting and enhancing the rights and interests of the indigenous Fijian community. Clear constitutional provisions are laid down for affirmative action to reduce ethnic disparities within a specified time frame.

> Not surprisingly, Fiji's Constitution is hailed internationally as an exemplary model for the protection and advancement of indigenous rights. These measures go well beyond the provisions of the ILO Convention 169 (Indigenous and Tribal Peoples Convention) and the UN [Draft] Declaration on the Rights of Indigenous Communities.[40]

Nationalists obviously disagreed with this account, but did not present a reasoned or convincing case, relying instead on mere assertion. Further, they were unclear as to just what they meant by indigenous rights. This led Fijian chief and Assistant Minister in the People's Coalition Government, Adi Ema Tagicakibau, to issue them with a challenge.

Responding to a media question on the coup makers' claim that they had acted because the 1997 Constitution did not protect indigenous rights, she declared that 'people calling for supremacy of indigenous rights must define what they mean by this'. She also provided this food for thought:

> Fijians are no different from others in that we all want the same comforts of income, education for our children, a secure and stable livelihood. There is absolutely nothing indigenous about these; they are universal aspirations. I can assure you that the current crisis has hit most indigenous Fijians hard,

which also proves that we cannot exist in isolation from others. Neither can we build indigenous rights on the ashes of other groups.[41]

But critical reaction to nationalist demagoguery on indigenous rights was not just local. International condemnation was at least as forthright. The United Nations, British Commonwealth, European Union, South Pacific Forum and many governments decried the nationalists' attempt at subordinating universal human rights to indigenous rights.

One instance in November 2000 caused a stir and raised the ire of the nationalists. In an address at the University of the South Pacific in Suva, the New Zealand High Commissioner to Fiji, Tia Barrett, said: 'Those responsible for the upheavals in Fiji are yet to face justice, and it seems incredible that this has not been done, despite the wealth of information available.' He found disturbing the 'continued absence of democratic institutions in Fiji to express the will of the people'.[42] On the matter of indigenous rights, he said:

> What is difficult to accept in this dialogue on indigenous rights is the under-lying assumption that those rights are pre-eminent over other fundamental human rights. This cannot be so in today's world ... Nowhere is it written in any holy script that because you are indigenous, you have first rights over others in their daily lives. You should be respected and highly regarded as an indigenous person, but respect is earned, not obtained on demand.[43]

The Government, of course, attacked Barrett. For its efforts it was in turn criticised, and by Fijians no less. For Jone Dakuvula, a leading spokesperson for the CCF, Barrett's views were 'worth repeating and elaborating because he has credibility as a successful Maori who is knowledgeable about indigenous issues and does not brook the sort of nonsense we have been hearing from some Taukei nationalists'. An important implication of Barrett's statement was this:

> The fact that George Speight's supporters justify their act of treason on the basis of indigenous rights, does not now give the beneficiaries of the Speight-inspired coup (that is members of the Interim Administration) the right to

throw the 1997 Constitution and the Election result that it produced into the dustbin of history.[44]

This makes all the more significant the March 2001 ruling by the Court of Appeal that the 1997 Constitution had not been lawfully abrogated. The decision reaffirmed the supremacy of constitutional authority, the rule of law and the broad democratic parameters of governance in Fiji.

But the high hopes this produced were as misplaced as those that followed similar constitutional turning points in the turbulent past. The 1990 Constitution had raised Fijian nationalist expectations that Fijian supremacy was finally guaranteed. But a counter-action followed, a democratic struggle against the Constitution that led eventually to the new Constitution in 1997. Progressive forces in Fiji heaved a collective and expectant sigh of relief. At last democracy had triumphed over extremist nationalism.

But the pattern of action and counter-action reasserted itself. In the wake of the 1997 Constitution, nationalists again mobilised, their actions culminating this time in the crisis of 2000. Progressives counter-acted with a series of challenges that culminated in the Court of Appeal's 2001 decision. This sparked a third cycle of action and counter-action. Nationalist pressures forced the President to formally sack Mahendra Chaudhry as Prime Minister, dissolve Parliament, and reinstate Qarase's Interim Administration as a caretaker government ahead of fresh elections later in the year.

The nationalist agenda remains unchanged. It forms the very first proposal in Qarase's Blueprint for Fijian Development:

> [The] preparation of a new Constitution to be promulgated on 24 July 2001 (Constitution Day) to give effect to the collective desire of Fijians that the national leadership positions of Head of State and Head of Government should always be held by them ... The point is stressed that it will be a new Constitution.

This story of recent political action and counter-action concerning Fiji's constitutions is important because it underlines the widely-held but misplaced belief that somehow a Constitution itself will deliver on hopes and expectations. The cycle of action and counter-action described above strongly suggests it will not, no matter what protections it affords. This is the lesson both the 1990 and 1997 Constitutions afford. Both protected indigenous rights but could not, of course, resolve the indigenous question. We could argue that no Constitution should be expected to. After all, these are matters for politicians to resolve. But Constitutions do establish the landscape in which politicians act, and both the 1990 and 1997 Constitutions deliberately perpetuated the old racial divisions that lie at the heart of Fiji's problems.

Our argument is that constitutionalism, by itself, does not provide a solution to Fiji's problems. Much more is needed. Basic assumptions, attitudes, institutions, policies and practices need to change. This is especially true in relation to the indigenous question. Prime responsibility for change lies with Fijians themselves for two reasons: one, many of the causes of Fijian disaffection lie within their own communities, institutions and leaderships; and two, many Fijians, especially nationalists, do not take kindly to criticism of things Fijian, especially by non-Fijians. This is not to suggest that non-Fijians should not engage in the debate, but rather that the debate is more likely to be effective if Fijians take the initiative and a leading role in it.

The way forward to resolving the indigenous question could usefully begin with a reconsideration of indigenousness: what it means, how it has been used, and how it affects the vital issues of basic human rights, identity, governance and economic development. From this examination might emerge better pointers to more effective strategies for addressing the indigenous question and, beyond that, to produce a more harmonious, inclusive and prosperous Fiji. The next chapter is a contribution to that task.

Chapter 4

Key issues for the future

IN THIS BOOK WE have argued that at the heart of Fiji's problems lies the indigenous question. Because it is tied to the wider dynamics of race relations and cultural diversity, the indigenous question can only be resolved through the cooperation of all Fiji's communities. However, Fijians have a special responsibility to take the initiative because for many years indigenous supremacy has been promoted as the only way to resolve the question. Today many Fijians regard it as an article of faith. Consequently, if there is to be a circuit breaker, we cannot expect it to emerge from Fiji's other communities, many of which remain intimidated by Fiji's political violence. It must come from Fijians.

But nothing will change until Fijians look honestly and critically at their own communities, traditions, institutions and leadership, and pay particular attention to the plight of their disadvantaged members. Without critical self-reflection, the mantra of supremacy will remain to frustrate their interests and aspirations, and they will fail to use Fiji's cultural diversity to their, and everyone else's, advantage.

To assist in this sensitive but crucial task, we now draw together the main threads of our discussion around the central theme of indigenousness and offer an initial but by no means exhaustive list of matters that need to be addressed.

INDIGENOUSNESS: MEANING AND USES

Indigenousness appears at first sight to be a relatively simple and straight-forward concept. But as we have shown, it is extremely problematic. In the first place, there is no internationally agreed meaning. Second, while it is used to describe aboriginal peoples, the first inhabitants, it is not always clear who precisely are, or can claim to be, aboriginal. Third, it is at least arguable that through birth and residence non-aboriginal peoples can legitimately claim to be native of their country. Fourth, the whole notion of aboriginal identity has been manipulated by elites in the pursuit of their agendas. In the case of Fiji, all of these features of indigenousness apply.

First, and foremost, indigenousness is part of the rhetoric of paramountcy which has been used as justification for supremacy over Fiji's non-indigenous peoples, most especially Indians. 'Fijians have only one motherland and father-land, and that is Fiji,' declared Interim Prime Minister Laisenia Qarase in the middle of 2000, and his words are echoed by many Fijian nationalists.[1] The cultures of Indians, Chinese and peoples of European descent find expres-sion elsewhere in the world, but Fijians only have Fiji, the land God dedicated for them alone. Thus Fiji's Indians are forever condemned as foreigners.

Second, the way in which many Fijians use the term indigenousness implies a degree of homogeneity that Fijians do not in fact enjoy. Fijians are themselves the products of internal and external migrations over several thousand years. Only colonialism brought them together as a single people but, as we saw in Chapter 2, it did so within a racial context defined largely by European colonists obsessed with securing their own future.

This colonial chimera of homogeneity bolstered claims for Fijian para-mountcy, but it also made more difficult accommodating difference within and between Fijian communities. By the 1990s Fijian differences in terms of wealth, place of origin and ethnic background increasingly gave the lie to the notion of Fijian homogeneity and led many nationalists to insist on racial purity as the basis for indigenousness. Others clamoured for provin-cial rights ahead of indigenous rights. Neither response served Fijians well in an era of rapid urbanisation and multiculturalism.

Third, indigenousness has also been defined by the long-standing struggle to maintain chiefly relevance in a vastly changing world. It has suited the chiefs to fossilise Fijianness within a tradition of relationships that placed chiefs and their associated elite at the apex. Not surprisingly many chiefs, like Naitasiri's Qaranivalu, looked back nostalgically on colonialism as a golden age. They believed that Fijians would be better off if colonial practices were reinstated. Fijians were like children; they needed 'to work within laws and regulations to keep them in order'.[2] By this means, also, criticism of economic policies of Fijian-dominated governments could be stifled. More generally, to criticise chiefs was to criticise Fijianness itself, and that now includes their institutions such as the Great Council of Chiefs, the Native Land Trust Board, even Fijian Holdings Ltd.

Today Fijian indigenousness contains a class agenda. Any attack on the Interim Government's Blueprint, declared Ratu Inoke Kubuabola, 'is really an attack on and an insult to indigenous Fijians'.[3] Indigenousness is rightly a source of pride. Sadly, it continues to be abused by extremists and self-interested elites to the detriment of Fiji's development generally and disadvantaged Fijians in particular.

INDIGENOUSNESS AND HUMAN RIGHTS

Since the mid-1990s Fijian nationalists have linked indigenousness with indigenous rights. International law recognises that indigenous peoples have rights. For example, they have the right to maintain their cultures and identities. But the precise scope and content of those rights have yet to be agreed. What is more, Fijian nationalists are unclear about the status of indigenous rights in international human rights law. But the one thing that law is clear about is that indigenous rights do not override universal human rights. Indigenous people can claim indigenous rights and press for their implementation, but they cannot do this to the detriment of the basic and universal human rights of others. In Fiji, unfortunately, nationalists wrongly equate indigenous rights with indigenous supremacy.

Fortunately, not all Fijians 'lack a real appreciation of what the world expects of them now', to quote Sir Paul Reeves, the Maori leader of the team that produced the 1997 Constitution.[4] There are, for example, Fijian members and supporters of Fiji's Human Rights Commission and non-governmental organisations that have worked tirelessly to promote the paramountcy of universal human rights — organisations like the Citizens Constitutional Forum, the Blue Day Committee, Social Action for Human Rights Aspirations (SAHARA), the Fiji Women's Rights Movement, the Fiji First Movement and the Fiji Women's Crisis Centre. According to one analysis, the Fiji Appeal Court's historic decision of March 2001 'exposed the strength of Fiji's non-government organisations'.[5] Many of these organisations had worked together to assist an Indian farmer who fled to a refugee camp to escape the terror his rural community experienced and whose legal challenge began the process that eventually led to the court's decision. As one NGO director put it, 'It goes to show what civil society can do in the developing world.'[6] Indeed, but the lesson remains to be absorbed by the nationalists.

INDIGENOUSNESS AND IDENTITY

The uses and abuses of indigenousness have had their greatest impact on national identity. Fijians took for themselves the country's national name; Fiji's other communities had to be content with ethnic descriptions. Even attempts by Indians to call themselves Indo Fijians have been rejected. Instead of gaining a national identity, Fiji's citizens have been boxed into separate identities.

The history of compartmentalising Fiji's population into ethnic groups needs to be undone. It perpetuates the wrong impression of homogenous and incompatible blocs. Indians, for example, are not a race; the term instead denotes nationality. In Fiji's case it applies to peoples who belong to or are derived from the nation of India. These peoples came from a number of widely differing provinces. They left at a time when the contemporary concept of India as a nation was in its infancy. Consequently, the

Indians who came to Fiji were not a singular or united people. Ethnicity, religion, caste, place of origin, and language divided them. Once in Fiji their indenture (*Girmit*) or free settler status also divided them. Ironically, what transcended those divisions for the settlers and their descendants were their colonial and post-colonial experiences of racism and communalism, not an already established sense of identity. By virtue of birth and residence, the descendants were natives of Fiji. They became Indo Fijians and, despite the provocation of 1987 and 2000, they consistently and rightly insisted on this.

Fijians are also divided. They are divided by commoner and chiefly status, by ethnic origin, by language and geography. Such divisions are not always sharp, but they exist nonetheless and, as we have noted, assumed new characteristics under colonialism and post-colonialism. The myth of a homogeneous indigenous community hid the reality of disunity. By promoting racial divisions, political authorities in Fiji hoped to elevate forms of unity that served their own narrow purposes. For colonial administrations, racial divisions reduced the possibility of united anti-colonial movements. Chiefs were similarly motivated. They wanted to reclaim leadership for themselves in the changing social and economic landscape.

This reality of heterogeneity is also true of Fiji's other communities. The impression and talk of homogenous communities is simply wrong. Equally important, the reality of life in Fiji gives the lie to the alleged incompatibility of communities, most especially Fijians and Indians. Certainly colonialism segregated people in their places of work, in the suburbs in which they lived and in the schools. Religious and linguistic differences reinforced the image of segregation, but in reality all Fiji's peoples contributed to a single economy and they all lived within the bounds of a comparatively small nation.

By the time colonialism ended, the artificial constraints were already collapsing and 30 years of decolonisation and urbanisation reinforced the trend. Workplaces, suburbs and schools became increasingly multiracial; so too did the places where people socialise. All Fiji's communities have been transformed by interaction. For example, many Indians speak Fijian, drink kava in a Fijian way, enjoy Fijian *lovo* food, and wear *sulus*. A small proportion has converted to Methodism.

Of course, exactly the same is true of Fijians and 'Fijian' culture. Vastly changed over the past century, they have been greatly influenced by British, Australasian, and Indian cultures. Indeed all Fiji's peoples, like people in most countries, are integrated into and influenced by growing global cultures which are experienced through the media, education, and professional, military, business and political associations. No better examples might be proffered than coup leaders Ilisoni Ligairi and George Speight, both of whom spent most of their adult lives away from Fiji. Such dynamism does not make Fijians any less indigenous, but it does demonstrate how much they share in common with their fellow citizens.

Ten years after he staged his 1987 coups, Sitiveni Rabuka told Parliament that what people held in common was more important than what divided them: 'It is not enough that we should accept our collective presence in Fiji as simply one of coexistence; we should accept each other as belonging together as one people and one nation.'[7] Two weeks earlier, Jai Ram Reddy, then leader of the largest Indian political party, made a similarly impassioned plea to the Great Council of Chiefs.

> The Indians of Fiji, brought to these shores as labourers, did not come to conquer or to colonise. We have no wish . . . to separate ourselves from you. Fiji is our home. We have no other. We want no other.[8]

Ratu Sir Kamisese Mara also conceded this after the Coalition victory in 1999. Indians 'may have a distinct and different appearance and characteristics and been late arrivals', he said, 'but islanders they are'.[9]

Clearly, then, the exclusive application of indigenousness to Fijians hurts Fiji enormously. It offends the legitimate claims and aspirations of other Fiji citizens who are natives of Fiji and denies commonalities between Fijians and non-Fijians. It frustrates the development of a national identity and therefore is a major obstacle to nation building. It stands in the way of Fijian advancement.

INDIGENOUSNESS AND GOVERNANCE: TRADITION AND DEMOCRACY

The dynamics of race in Fiji have tended to overshadow issues of good governance. Indeed many indigenous nationalists have asserted that democracy is a Western invention unsuitable for traditional societies like Fiji. Central to this argument is the belief in a fundamental dichotomy between tradition and modernity. Understanding the basic fallacy of this belief is as important for Fiji's future welfare as dismantling the racial categories that have so divided the nation. But in reaching such an understanding we need first to appreciate that the dichotomy is not only symptomatic of a world view (with an appeal that goes far beyond Fiji's shores) but also a crucial element in Fijian identity.

At one level the dichotomy between tradition and modernity is presented as a struggle, something 'culturally and structurally deep-seated . . . that confronts communal societies everywhere as they struggle to adjust their values and social practices to the relentless demands and myriad opportunities of the modern world'.[10] The struggle defines them. 'We, the indigenous, have been brought up in a traditional manner, not democratic manner which is part of the Western culture,' argues Takiveikata, the Qaranivalu of Naitasiri. 'Fijians don't know much about democracy and free living.'[11]

This is also Qarase's view: 'Loyalty, obedience, mutual care and sharing rather than . . . equality of rights and privileges, or acquiring . . . material wealth, [these] are the values [Fijians] treasure most.'[12]

> We all welcome democracy in laying importance on the equal rights of individuals, their equality before the law, and a system of government and leadership based on the consent of the people, and not on divine right or status at birth. But in the long run, it will also serve to undermine chiefly status and authority in our traditional society. And the collective value systems that bind us together as a community.[13]

Qarase's message is unambiguous. Democracy is Western. It is a foreign flower. It is irrelevant to local traditions and disadvantages already marginalised people. It renders self-determination meaningless.

The idea of an overwhelming dichotomy between tradition and modernity has widespread international currency. Three constitutions have failed in Fiji, says Australian academic Robert Wolfgramm, because they were unable to satisfy two completely different sets of values, one Western, the other Fijian. By opting for Western values, Fiji nearly lost 'its indigenous soul'. The solution is plain: a future constitution must restore Fijian paramountcy.[14] New Zealand Foreign Minister Phil Goff might not agree with Wolfgramm's remedy, but he certainly agrees with the diagnosis. 'Clearly grafting a Western system of government on to a chiefly system of government,' he believes, 'has not worked.'[15]

Canadian academic John Davies accepts the dichotomy also. He writes of the 'difficulty confronted by a traditional, subsistence society in adapting to a modern market economy and the values, economic imperatives and modes of thought that sustain it'. But he argues the difference in Fiji's case is that 'the Indian presence robs Fijians' of the 'luxury of managing this transition at their own pace'.[16] The *Australian*'s foreign editor, Greg Sheridan, positions the conflict within Fiji's institutions themselves.

> Its institutions are weak. [Fiji] has so far not made the transition from a traditional to a modern society. Its institutions are pale imitations of Western institutions. They haven't taken root, they are not well adapted culturally, they are often staffed by people somewhat removed from their own cultures. They cope very poorly under stress.[17]

All these comments exaggerate distinctions. They see a dichotomy where none exists.

Tradition is not reasserting itself. No traditional institutions survive in contemporary Fiji. Certainly institutions like the Great Council of Chiefs are presented as traditional. But they are, in fact, modern institutions. They originated as centralised instruments for colonial control but quickly transformed themselves into instruments for the assertion of chiefly authority. And they operate entirely within a contemporary milieu. Tradition that the chiefs claim to represent is simply a mask obscuring their very contemporary struggle to dominate the development agenda.

Yet our responses to this contradiction are usually ambiguous. Often we draw falsely on the past to lend legitimacy to our perceptions of modern institutions. We argue that democracy is a Western invention that derived from Greek experiments millennia ago. Or we celebrate its origins in the English Magna Carta. This is no different from Qarase's selective use of the past to justify bestowing on the Great Council of Chiefs new political functions.

> Chiefs derive their legitimate authority from their position in the indige-
> nous Fijian social hierarchy from time immemorial and which was confirmed
> in the recognition given to them in the Deed of Cession, 10 October 1874.
> This gives the Great Council of Chiefs legal superiority and the right to
> appoint governments.[18]

These kinds of responses make it easy for us to overlook the fact that democracies everywhere are very recent and often fragile forms of government that developed only as societies became more complex and as popular struggles won greater equality for their citizens and demanded accountability from their governments. It is in this very modern struggle that Fiji finds itself today.

Institutions that we often regard as traditional are part of that modern struggle, in much the same way as militaries, corporations and bureaucracies are. None of them are static or unchanging. They all seek greater influence, and contribute to the ongoing tension within democracies. Certainly so-called traditional institutions in Fiji, like the Great Council of Chiefs, the Provincial Councils or the Native Land Trust Board, are dynamic institutions. They respond to changing social and political realities around them. In the past 20 years alone they have undergone significant changes and their roles have been transformed dramatically. This is not to say that they always work as effectively as they should. But the problems they confront are not derived from a dichotomy between tradition and modernity.

Nor are they derived from the inability of Fijians to 'dictate their own pace of change', as Adi Samanunu Cakobau declared back in 1995.[19] No peoples have ever been able to adapt in a manner and pace directed solely by themselves. The widespread discontent generated by so-called global-isation over the past 20 years is but one contemporary example of this reality. Nor are Fijian problems due in any way to the modernity of Indians compared with the tradition of Fijians. Qarase once argued that India's long history of trade and industry gave Fiji's Indians an unfair advantage over Fijians.[20] But this is not true in at least two different ways.

First, most of Fiji's Indian migrants were poor peasants or townspeople displaced by colonial transformation. Even today, as we have seen, Indians form at least half of the country's poor. To blame Indians for reinforcing a tradition/modernity divide is simply to employ the very generalisations and stereotypes that reinforce division and distrust. Their effect is to strengthen belief in collective failure and cultural backwardness; in other words, they generate among Fijians the victim syndrome.

Second, Fijians have a history of trade and exchange that has been largely ignored. In fact, Fiji once formed a central part of a vast trans-Pacific network. But this knowledge about themselves has been lost, and today many Fijians believe they were 'uncivilised' before Europeans arrived. This has made it easier for many people – Fijians and non-Fijians alike – to talk about Fijian economic backwardness and to blame it on Fijian culture.

In fact Fijian institutions need look no further than at their own perfor-mance to find causes for their difficulties. Nepotism, cronyism and colonial-style command structures all derive from a corporate culture that disregards transparency, dialogue and accountability. This issue has rarely been tackled in Fiji, at least with regard to Fijian institutions. Instead, Fijian discontent tends to focus on leadership, not governance.

Colonel Filipo Tarakinikini, for example, blames the post-war leadership for failing to groom a new generation of chiefs to assume the roles they clearly covet.[21] But other Fijians argue that chiefs should never have sought those roles in the first place. Tupeni Baba blames the Great Council of Chiefs for becoming obsessed with restoring Fijian unity and the role of chiefs within Fijian society at any cost. It supported the 1987 coups to that end and transformed itself into an elite body of senior chiefs with the power to appoint Presidents and half the Senate.

The Great Council of Chiefs also formed its own political party, the SVT, to govern the nation on its behalf.[22] According to Adi Kuini Vuikaba, herself a former member of the Council, such politicisation weakened the institution. Fijians who supported rival political parties failed to show it the deference it expected. They regarded it as a refuge for SVT supporters, not as an august body of senior chiefs.[23] In the 1999 elections, two-thirds of Fijians voted against the chiefs' party. Exit polls suggested only 9 per cent of Fijians were influenced by the wishes of their chiefs.

Facing such a momentous rejection, many chiefs desperately latched on to the CRWU rebels as an opportunity to regain lost ground. This is certainly how many nearby Tongans viewed events. 'Chiefs are embroiled in plots and intrigue to ensure that he/she will reap the rewards craved, for which all principles have been discarded', observed journalist Sione Masina.[24] 'In such a climate of trendy racism', Crown Prince Tupouto'a concurred, 'we should not at all be surprised that common thugs such as Speight and his fellow traitors are able to justify treason with blatant racism.'[25] The same applies to many of the chiefs, but what provided the latter with most scope for such action was the failure of their institutions to insist on basic principles of accountability and transparency.

Accordingly, we argue that it is unhelpful to explain the problems facing Fijians (and in particular those that lie at the heart of the 2000 crisis) in terms of Fiji's failure to manage the tensions between tradition and modernity. To do so relies on a vague, ambiguous and fallacious dichotomy. Opportunism, class agendas, the failure of multiracialism to end the racial divides that colonialism had found so convenient, the projection of Fijian elite interests as representing indigenous paramountcy, and the failure of Fijian-dominated governments and institutions to redress the disadvantage of ordinary Fijians – these are the major reasons for Fijian problems, not the threat of Indian dominance, not Fiji's lack of modernity, not its incompatibility with democracy, and certainly not weaknesses in its Constitution.

The history of Fiji since independence demonstrates that democracy in Fiji is dynamic. It is not a foreign and imposed concept but the result of forces largely indigenous to Fiji. Fiji's soil is fertile because Fiji society is just as multicultural as it is multiracial. With so many conflicting identities and allegiances, only some form of democracy can hope to create the kind of national unity Fiji craves; or the kind of accountable and transparent environment necessary for the free flow of information and ideas, responsible decision making, human development and creativity. Democracy is a prerequisite for sustainable development, for equity and accountability.

Fiji made considerable steps in coming to terms with this reality. Its new Constitution established structures designed to reduce appeals to race and instead promote tolerance and respect for human rights. For the first time in Fiji's history, a Constitution deliberately set out to strengthen civil society organisations and to effect greater popular participation in governance. Women gained equal citizenship rights to men. Sexual discrimination became illegal. A Human Rights Commission was established, a Bill of Rights enacted, a Compact of Understanding set out clearly the indigenous rights of Fijians, and government decision making became more open to parliamentary scrutiny. These were all very positive developments.

Nonetheless, fears remained that the new Constitution had not sufficiently departed from the kind of racial categorisation that promoted zero sum perceptions. It called everyone 'Fiji Islanders' for the first time, but it did not make the old boundaries between Indians and Fijians more fluid or encourage more inclusive identities. The old 'us' and 'them' mind-set remained. Nor did it seek to impose on Fijian institutions the same standards of accountability, transparency and equity it determined essential for the nation as a whole. Thus the Great Council of Chiefs remained an institution shrouded in secrecy. Its deliberations are never open to public scrutiny.

Similarly many very important institutions designed to promote the welfare of Fijians are rarely subject to public audit. Set up as guardians of Fijian interests, they have regularly abused that trust. The Native Land Trust Board, which asked Fijians to transfer all their lands to it in a Deed of

Sovereignty for the rebel Taukei Civilian Government, has failed to manage Fijian land affairs in an open and professional manner. In addition, its practice of making all decisions on behalf of landowners not only smacks of colonial paternalism but also distances landowners from economic participation and deprives them of skills they might otherwise have acquired. Consequently it shares responsibility for many of the grievances voiced by rural Fijians and in no small measure contributed to the 2000 crisis. Similar complaints might be laid against the managers of the National Bank of Fiji, whose practices of cronyism plunged Fiji into recession after 1995, and against the Fiji Development Bank.

If Fijian institutions had not acted in the way they did, the CRWU rebels would never have been able to exploit rural Fijian disaffection to such telling effect against the Fijian establishment in 2000. Fiji cannot avoid this conclusion. Simply dismissing democracy as a Western concept unsuited to traditional indigenous societies and institutions is to deny indigenous peoples the right to accountability, transparency and equity, the foundations of any form of sustainable development. This is certainly how Frank Bainimarama at one time interpreted Fijian discontent in 2000. It was not about Indians, but about good governance. 'People are frustrated about the way they have been governed over the years', he claimed.[26]

But there is another conclusion that also needs to be drawn. The 2000 crisis was not a consequence of the 1997 Constitution. It derived instead from Fijian perceptions of disadvantage. To address that requires transforming economic strategies of development that have marginalised further the majority of Fiji's indigenous peoples.

But on this matter of governance, our analysis leads to the following key point. The 1997 Constitution was not the cause of the 2000 crisis and was in fact a major step towards better governance. But the inordinate faith that continues to be placed on it as the answer to Fiji's problems generally and the indigenous question in particular is misguided. Certainly it helps, but much more important is the need to change the economic strategies that have marginalised the majority of Fiji's peoples, including the politically most critical group – the ordinary, disadvantaged Fijians.

INDIGENOUSNESS, ECONOMIC DEVELOPMENT AND EDUCATION

Fiji's economic strategies have been based on the premise that the Fiji economy can be segregated. That premise is false in two important ways. First, Fijian and Indian economic activities are entwined. Fijian welfare depends upon Indian economic participation and investment. And vice versa. Second, no one exists outside of the mainstream economy, not even Fijians within the so-called traditional milieu. Communal obligations cost money. So does education. And no one has escaped the onslaught of what is termed globalisation, the growth of large-scale, centralised, foreign-owned businesses. The stubborn persistence in Fiji of the false subsistence economy/modern economy dichotomy has fostered a victim mentality among many Fijians and made more difficult the resolution of important economic issues, such as land usage.

Of course, that dichotomy draws inspiration from Fiji's homogenising stereotypes. Thus Indians are said to dominate the economy, an argument paraded constantly during 2000 (as it had been in 1987) to reinforce the idea of Fijian disadvantage. The fact that transnationals dominate the Fiji economy, in some instances in partnership with Fijian corporate interests, rarely disturbs the mythology promoted. Also similar are assertions that Indians are wealthier than Fijians. Interim Prime Minister Qarase, for example, argues that Fijians on average receive lower incomes than Indians, but the poverty reports of the 1990s all contradict him. Slightly more Indians live in poverty than Fijians, and for both Indians and Fijians the great majority (two-thirds) live in rural areas.

Again this reality contradicts one of the important myths generated before and during the crisis; that poor Fijians were being disadvantaged by the refusal of wealthy Indians to accept the revision of farm leases. Controversy over land arose, as we noted earlier, because of Native Land Trust Board mismanagement and because Fiji failed to reorganise a farming system that relied too heavily on peasant agriculture. These were not new issues, but in the politically charged atmosphere of the times the stereotype of the greedy Indian made it easy to overlook the fact that, on average, cane production netted farmers annual incomes under $4,000. Land rentals averaged $1,300 per year.[27]

For the last 10 years this largely racially driven debate has completely overshadowed a much more important issue, land usage. Fiji's main revenue earner — the sugar industry — depends for its survival on continued access to preferential markets in regions such as Europe. That access is now under threat. With many of Fiji's cane farms too small to effect the kinds of productivity gains needed to survive in more competitive markets, and with many farms occupying marginal land, Fiji needs to plan seriously the future of its vitally important farming sector. Indians might dominate the farming sector, but sugar returns more income to the country as a whole than virtually any other economic sector. Its loss would devastate all Fiji, not just Indians. Unfortunately the racial focus obscures both this reality and the need for a more realistic national strategy for the difficult economic times ahead.

But there is another aspect to Fiji's economic and social strategies that Fiji's leaders should address, and that is the elite bias inherent in policies paraded as benefiting all Fijians. As we noted in Chapter 3, Qarase's proposals for Fijian affirmative action are not new. They represent the intensification of a form of communal capitalism that Fiji has pursued since independence. After 1970, Fijian resources were collectively marshalled to support chiefly and bureaucratic elites, often themselves in alliance with leading foreign and local capitalists. Such policies did not liberate Fijian initiative, with the result that even as late as 1995 some 62 per cent of rural Fijians depended entirely upon subsistence agriculture for their survival.[28] Nonetheless, after the 1987 coups, these policies were repackaged with great fanfare to benefit the corporate interests of a small number of well-connected Fijian bureaucrats and chiefs.

Qarase sees nothing wrong in this. Elites possess 'vision, initiative and innovation', he argues. 'They should be encouraged because they are often the people that drive a country forward.'[29] Yet the record demonstrates the opposite. Elite-driven initiatives deprived Fijians of resources and drove the rural poor into cities in record numbers after 1987. Indeed, by the mid-1990s the corruption these initiatives generated pushed Fiji into recession and was in no small measure responsible for Rabuka's constitutional about-turn in 1997. Yet in the midst of the 2000 crisis, at the very moment when Ligairi employed his rural and peri-urban disaffected Fijians against the military and against the chiefs, Qarase resurrected the same policies and called them The Blueprint for Fijian Development. Why? Because it is the only strategy which both reinforces the economic status quo and mobilises Fijians ethnically behind traditional leaders and their allies.[30]

The Blueprint promises much for this elite: leadership training, a national savings scheme to increase corporate investments, tax exemptions for Fijian companies, complete autonomy for government-funded Fijian institutions, the conversion of an earlier $20 million government loan to Fijian Holdings Ltd into a grant, and the creation of a new interest-free loan to another Fijian holding company. But it promises nothing for the disadvantaged Fijian majority. Certainly it dwells on water rights, the transfer of Crown land, and increases in land rentals, but few of these matters impact on the daily life of Fijians. With half of all rental incomes going directly to bureaucracies like the Native Land Trust Board or to chiefs, the remaining sums are rarely marshalled in ways that assist commoner Fijians.

Although the Blueprint considers education a priority, it outlines no new strategy to lift rural schools from their depressed state; nor to address associated problems faced by students at home where space for study is limited and where scarce resources are often diverted to church or *vanua* activities (including the funding of Qarase's communal capitalism) rather than paying off school fees or purchasing books. Indeed, Fiji's education system notoriously leaves communities themselves to resource most schools. Thus poor communities invariably have poorly resourced and maintained schools. Their children are more likely to be malnourished. Their dropout and absenteeism rates are higher; their exam results consistently poorer. 'Rather than reducing vulnerability to poverty,' one educationalist wrote, 'the present education system may exacerbate it by multiplying the disadvantages of lower socio-economic groups.'[31]

Education is but one demonstration of the poverty of Fijian nationalism's economic strategies, perhaps revealed more starkly now than at any time in the past. In the 1980s several large rural Fijian schools experimented with forms of multiracial education and were successful in significantly raising educational standards and student performance. But these experiments ran counter to official wishes to immerse students in the traditions of their *vanua* instead, and have only Fijians teach Fijians. They were ended, and indigenous Fijians suffered as a result.[32] The same dilemma now more starkly faces Fijians in the wake of the 2000 crisis. It is an issue Fiji's leaders must address if the nation is to move forward.

DEVELOPING THE NATION: AN INITIATIVE FOR THE FUTURE

Drawing the threads together indicates more clearly the challenges now facing indigenous Fijians and the practical steps Fiji must take if recovery is ever to be possible. Past strategies to address the indigenous question and, more generally, to manage cultural diversity, have failed. Our analysis suggests the need for practical strategies focussing on identity, affirmative action, Fijian institutions and education to emerge from addressing the indigenous question. Similarly, strategies focussing on human rights, governance and democracy emerge from the wider but related task of more effectively managing cultural diversity.

Instead of yet another constitutional review, we propose a much broader review of the nation as part of a 'Developing the Nation' initiative to focus Fiji's attention on the problems which lie behind its current crisis. 'Developing the Nation' would have a number of different parts, each serviced by committees with greater civil society representation than has usually been the case in the past. One part should develop a study of Fijian history; another should examine the question of nationality; a third the economy and resource distribution; and a fourth the revamping of state and indigenous institutions. Such a 'Developing the Nation' initiative would be a more positive and encompassing way to move forward than a narrowly focussed constitutional review or even a truth commission, neither of which can themselves address the issues that lie behind Fijian dissatisfaction. Within such an initiative the following issues, among others, need to be addressed. We have divided these into two broad categories, the first having more specifically to do with what Fijians can do to address the indigenous question, the second with wider nation-building issues.

ADDRESSING THE INDIGENOUS QUESTION

1. Understand the meaning and history of indigenousness

Fijians need to be clear as to the meaning of indigenousness and the purpose of indigenous identification. Does indigenousness imply aboriginality? If so, how significant is aboriginality in defining Fijianness, especially given the fact that Fijian political dominance since independence has failed to maintain Fijian unity. Many Fijian leaders and chiefs are at a loss to explain disunity, and regard Indian threats as a cause. With Indians 'neutralised', they expected Fijian differences to dissolve, forgetting of course that historically Fijians have never been a homogenous and united people.

Fijians have still to learn that history, and it is one of the central tasks Fiji must set itself. Fijians must learn their unsanitised history, not the history constructed by colonial officials or the history produced by postcolonial elites. Until then Fiji will remain blind to the causes of Fijian disaffection, many of which — like the differences between western and eastern Fiji — lie within its own communities. Not only that, without an honest history Fijians will continue to undervalue their past. They will never learn of the dynamism that permitted their people to survive the great changes their societies underwent during and after colonialism. Instead they will remain trapped within a false consciousness of indigenousness as marginality and victimhood.

2. Disconnect indigenous rights from indigenous supremacy and unity

Indigenous rights do not equate with indigenous supremacy or unity. To suggest otherwise risks promoting forms of authoritarianism that will deny basic human rights in Fiji and prevent the realisation of indigenous rights.

This happened after 1987 when Rabuka deemed that Fijians were not ready for democracy and needed a strong government to guide their development.

Today the argument has shifted a little, but its implications are still the same. During his inauguration as President in March 2001, Ratu Iloilo declared that 'the ultimate guarantee of the . . . paramountcy of Fijian inter-ests lies . . . in the political unity of Fijians themselves'.[33] But as his predecessor once recognised, only dictatorship could ever hope to achieve unity among Fijians.[34] That prospect – according to the Roko Tui Bau, Ratu Jone Madraiwiwi – still does not deter 'a particular group of Fijians' who use unity as 'an excuse . . . to sustain themselves in power'.[35]

Fijians are no different from anyone else in requiring an open environ-ment in which to achieve their full creative potential. Consequently every effort must be made by government and the people to counteract the promotion of indigenous supremacy and its corollaries.

3. Share national identity

Indigenous identity cannot be claimed at the expense of other identities, least of all a national identity. Fijians have captured for themselves the national name. If Fiji is to prosper, it can only do so as one nation, with Fijians of all cultures working together to create a transformed and vibrant society. Calling everybody by the same name is a first step in overcoming the legacies of colonialism and moving forward. It tells everybody they belong, that they are equal, and that they are valued as people and indi-viduals. Thus the indigenous people of Fiji could become known as *i taukei*, the non-indigenous as *vasu* if an inclusive term is required. This would be an enormously powerful gesture with which to begin the process of healing and reconciliation. This matter requires urgent attention and should be a crucial component of the 'Developing The Nation' initiative.

4. Devolve Fijian decision making

Indigenous institutions need to be re-examined because of their centrality to the indigenous question. If institutions like the Great Council of Chiefs and the Native Land Trust Board are to serve their people well and be cost effective, they must be transparent and open in their operations and account-able for them. They must also shake off their centralised colonial roles and devolve decision making to Provincial Councils and, above all, to *mataqali* and villages, especially in relation to the economic use of land and other resources. Too often they treat their people like children and deprive them of opportunities to increase their business and decision-making skills. Instead indigenous institutions must respect the rights of their people and bear responsibility for their actions. As one Fijian sociologist argued, 'In the long run a democratic society cannot come about unless you democratise Fijian society.'[36]

5. Ensure greater respect for the rule of law by Fijian institutions

Fijian institutions must strive to empower, not rule like fiefdoms. Like the citizens they serve, they must also heed the rule of law. Since the 2000 attempted coup, the Great Council of Chiefs has acted as if it is more than an advisory body; that it is, in effect, above the law. Many Fijian officials apparently accept its extra-legal status. When the Fiji Court of Appeal ruled the Constitutional Review Committee illegal, the President allowed it to continue its work. When the High Court demanded its dismissal, the President dismissed the Committee but contracted four of its commissioners to complete its report. Their mandate, said caretaker Prime Minister Qarase, came from the Great Council of Chiefs.[37] As lawyer Tupou Draunidalo warns, if institutions do not themselves observe the rule of law, 'there is nothing to ground the citizen to observe the rule of law'.[38] Indigenous insti-tutions like the Fiji Military Forces and the Great Council of Chiefs do not possess rights that supersede the law, as many nationalists argue. To accept such an argument opens Fiji to serial disasters.

6. Strengthen Fijian institutions with principles of transparency and accountability

Fiji must put aside the self-seeking rhetoric of traditionalism. Fiji is a modern nation. There is, as Jone Dakuvula notes, no choice between liberal democ-racy and chiefly rule. Chiefs – and perhaps also their *vanua* – will only survive by adopting 'modern principles of leadership and accountability'. The idea of Fijian political unity is a chimera. Pursuing it under the guise of indigenous rights produces its opposite – 'provincialism, parochialism, unhealthy rivalries, patronage, corruption and the discrediting of the chiefly system'.[39] It also reinforces a victim mentality from which it is difficult to escape.

Despite what extremist Fijian nationalists say, indigenousness is not incompatible with democracy. Basic democratic principles like those of accountability and transparency apply everywhere, and their relative weakness in Fiji makes their strengthening all the more important. They should therefore be explicitly built into the laws governing all Fiji's institutions, including indigenous ones.

7. Demonstrate that affirmative action benefits disadvantaged Fijians

The relationship between indigenousness and economic development needs to be re-examined. Affirmative action is a blunt instrument for indigenous development. The record suggests that affirmative action has most assisted individuals already in advantaged positions. Ligairi's dogs of war indicate to Fiji one possible future if it fails to address commoner development and effect even development. Again, equity, transparency and accountability are principles vitally important for indigenous welfare. If economic affirmative action is to continue, then the government must give account to taxpayers that their money has in fact been used to help economically disadvantaged Fijians. In practice this means, among other things:

(i) specifying the intended outcomes of all affirmative action programs;

(ii) in line with those outcomes, setting particular goals and targets to be achieved within specified timeframes;

(iii) identifying performance indicators and measures by which to assess program outcomes;

(iv) demonstrating that beneficiaries are in fact disadvantaged Fijians; and

(v) providing annual reports to the Parliament on all affirmative action programs.

BUILDING THE NATION

1. Celebrate and utilise cultural diversity

Fiji must change its use of generic racial categories – Fijian, Indian, European, Chinese and so on. We have suggested that the focus on race should be dropped. All Fijian citizens should be known as Fijians and, where differentiation is required, they should be referred to either as *i taukei* or *vasu*. But the use of these sub-national terms should be restricted, perhaps largely to matters dealing with indigenous rights and institutions. One reason for such a restriction is to allow Fiji to move away from the kind of stereotyping that has dogged it ever since colonisation. Indeed, all Fijians should be encouraged to recognise their diversity. They might be *i taukei* but they are also *Lauan, Bauan* or – given the extent of urbanisation – *kai Suva*. They are also Methodists, Catholics, Hindus or Moslems. And they are men and women.

Equally importantly, Fijians should be encouraged to recognise that they are more than just one thing; they have multiple identities. They may also have multiple heritages. Being *i taukei* should not mean denying European, Indian, Chinese, Pacific Island or other ancestry. Indigenous Fijians and other Fiji citizens should be allowed to celebrate their diverse backgrounds, and not be locked into exclusive categories.

2. Establish a national anti-racialism education program

More generally, Fiji needs to use its official resources to overcome the racist rhetoric which has been so much a feature of its social and political life, and develop a respect for human rights and cultural diversity. Racial rhetoric, like that of traditionalism, generates belief in collective Fijian failure, cultural backwardness and loss of control. Together they reduce Fiji's ability to exploit the uniqueness and dynamic of its own peoples; they retard national growth. The 1997 Constitution promised to lead Fiji in this direction, but as events have shown, much more is needed. A document alone cannot effect reconciliation and make Fiji more than just the sum of its many identities. It cannot end ingrained forms of racial vilification or the habit of blaming Indians for Fijian disadvantage. But acknowledging the past honestly and embarking on a national program of education will have more important long-term effects. At the very least it is an important first step.

3. Develop transcultural identities

Fiji needs to turn its attention to developing transcultural identities. The perception of two homogenous blocs, Fijians and Indians, confronting each other in competition for scarce resources is always likely to produce confrontation and animosity. On the other hand, recognising and accepting diversity based on gender, religion, language, place of origin, heritage and so on reduces this likelihood and opens up new ways in which Fiji might profit from its diversity and, hence, in time come to value it.

Diversity offers new opportunities in education, makes possible the acquisition of different language skills, and promotes a versatility that might open up regional and international opportunities. Accepted and respected, diversity will also offer visitors to Fiji a much richer experience. It will thereby provide the important tourism industry with a new platform from which to promote itself.

Of course, everyone in Fiji has a role to play in bringing about the changes in attitudes and behaviour required for cultural diversity to be valued and used to the country's advantage. But the state has a particularly special responsibility. Without a concerted effort on its part, the task will flounder as it has in the past. However, with state support there may emerge a transcultural national identity alongside Fiji's diverse cultural identities.

4. Strengthen civil society participation

Fiji needs to develop a strong civil society and encourage more open debate. With respect to Fijian institutions, we have recommended devolved decision making. Some Fijians have also suggested that establishing provincial governments might reduce the power of central government. But a system of provincial government is an expensive option for a small country and by itself cannot address Fiji's problems. It might simply provide another avenue for elite domination. In this regard Fiji can learn from countries like Papua New Guinea, Solomon Islands and Vanuatu, whose experience with provincial government has been less than satisfactory.

A more cost effective and socially inclusive strategy is to strengthen civil society participation in decision making. Public participation in policy processes can be easily increased through summits, parliamentary standing committees and other forms of public consultation. But public participation must be genuine, not token. The government must take it seriously and the public needs to be convinced of this. Government must ensure ample time and resources for preparation and engagement, access to necessary information, and that decisions are fully explained.

5. Change economic strategies for more equitable resource distribution

If there is only one lesson to be drawn from the crisis of 2000, it is the need for a massive redistribution of resources. This was the key message from Ligairi's 'dogs of war'. Large economic disparities make people angry and envious. Fiji's economic strategies have long had this effect. Changing them for more equitable outcomes will be very difficult, but necessary nonetheless for stability and progress.

There is no detailed blueprint for this task. It is something for the various interest groups to negotiate. But a useful start is for the government to set reasonable boundaries within which negotiations can take place. An obvious one is that nationalist aspirations must not compromise the national good. A second might be that state policy and resources be better used in part to ensure competition on a more equal footing.

In 1996 the authors of Fiji's constitutional review noted that progress is achieved only when 'citizens realise that what is good for their neighbour must ultimately be good for them as well, when difference and diversity are seen not as sources of division and distrust but of strength and inspiration'.[40] This is the challenge that still faces Fiji and its peoples.

For indigenous Fijians in particular, the challenge is not the absence of indigenous paramountcy, as many Fijian nationalists have asserted. Fijians are politically paramount, but paramountcy has brought them neither wealth nor unity. Similarly, the challenge is not to do with the incompatibility of democracy with tradition. Democracy is needed more than ever to ensure indigenous well-being. Nor is it even the impossibility of harmony in plural societies. Pluralism takes many forms and is just as capable of enriching societies as creating the basis for division.

In the year 2000 Ligairi and Speight once again showed Fiji what can happen when the challenge is not accepted. They also demonstrated how much harder the challenge becomes each time it is rejected. The question that remains unanswered is whether Fiji can free itself from the weight of past divisions and once more take up the challenge. As Fiji enters the new millennium, that is the indigenous question for the future, Fiji's unfinished business.

Postscript: the August 2001 elections

AS THIS BOOK WENT to press in September 2001, Fiji had just completed its elections. Before looking at the results of those elections, we need to say something briefly about the context in which they were held. First, while the President's call for elections signalled to the international community that Fiji is committed to democracy, it also served more immediately to prevent the restoration of Chaudhry's Coalition Government after the Fiji Court of Appeal declared the military's postcoup intervention illegal. Thus democratic practices could serve very undemocratic goals.

Second, the elections took place under conditions of continued instability and provocation. Fiji's military remains divided and its commitment to democracy and accountability in doubt. A published affidavit from its commander shortly before the August elections suggested that it would not accept Chaudhry's restoration as Prime Minister. At the same time, a Presidential decree granted amnesty to all military personnel for actions undertaken after their illegal assumption of power in late May 2000, including the brutal suppression of the mutineers and their CRWU colleagues.

Third, authorities have been tardy in bringing the perpetrators of the 2000 coup to justice. No investigation into the coup has ever been made public, and in August the Suva Magistrates Court even gave Speight and Ligairi permission to register as candidates in the forthcoming elections. Indeed most Fijian politicians have endorsed the latter's demands for absolute Fijian paramountcy, hoping to exploit Fijian nationalism to their own advantage. In this respect Qarase was not alone in attempting to ride the tiger of Fijian disenchantment by presenting the supremacist 1990 Constitution as a model for the future.

In terms of the case we have presented in this book, the key question is whether the election outcome will lead to a resolution of the indigenous question and assist Fiji to escape government by the gun. Our overall assessment is not optimistic. Indeed, Qarase's focus on a constitutional solution neatly underscores Fiji's continued failure to redress inequalities that foster political instability. Fiji's economy has changed dramatically since independence in 1970. But the changes have not been accompanied by the kind of popular economic participation that enables political stability. In the face of sharper class and rural–urban inequalities, politicians have consistently defended themselves by scapegoating, usually of the simplistic racial variety that colonial authorities once employed so effectively. In this regard the 2001 elections represented nothing new. Qarase presented indigenous rights and affirmative action programs to Fijians as the only solution available to them. He dismissed accusations that in the past such policies entrenched the privileges and wealth of the Fijian elite and left the majority of Fijians economically disadvantaged. Fijian survival depended upon Fijian unity, not class rhetoric.

Conducted under the shadow of the 2000 coup, the August 2001 elections did not enable dispassionate debate on strategies and outcomes. The Fiji Labour Party fought for the just restoration of its government, Qarase's new SDL for the continuation of its postcoup administration and policies, and the Conservative Alliance for the legitimization of the 2000 coup. Not surprisingly the results reflected this polarisation. Small Fijian parties like PANU, the FAP, and the VLV, which had comprised an important part of the People's Coalition Government, were routed. So too the new Bai Kei Viti and the once dominant SVT. The SVT's former leader, Kubuabola, lost his seat. Indeed Qarase's SDL nearly succeeded in winning all Fijian seats, its only rival being the new Conservative Alliance, which secured five seats in Vanua Levu and one in Tailevu (for George Speight). Indians similarly rallied behind the Fiji Labour Party; it won twenty-seven seats.

With thirty-one seats, Qarase had clearly defeated Labour and hoped to form a Fijian-dominated government either with the support of the Conservative Alliance or with a small group of minor parties and independents that had also won six seats (two for the NLUP, one for the GVP, one for the NFP and two independents). But immediately Qarase's ambitions were frustrated by the Constitution, which had been framed with quite different intentions in mind. It mandates power sharing. It requires that parties winning more than ten per cent of the seats be offered a proportionate number of seats in the cabinet. At the time of writing, Qarase had made such an offer to the Fiji Labour Party which it accepted. But Qarase then ignored the acceptance.

Qarase wanted his victory to herald a fourth period of post independence Fijian political domination, not the start of a new era of multiracial cooperation that the Constitution envisaged. Like Mara (1970–1987, the interim administration (1988–92) and Rabuka (1992–1999) before him, he represents elite Fijian interests that have consistently portrayed themselves as synonymous with those of ordinary Fijians. In the past, the inequalities generated by their policies fanned the flames of racial politics and promoted the perfect environment for elite advantage and military interventions. Qarase's future will have the same outcomes unless he addresses the problems facing ordinary Fijians and works within the multiracial spirit of the 1997 Constitution. So far the outcome of the 2001 elections does not inspire confidence. Once again the focus is on indigenous rights and Qarase's perception that the Constitution now frustrates those rights by preventing him from forming a solely Fijian Government. Fiji has not yet put the events of May 2000 behind it. Consequently it is too early to forecast an end to government by the gun in Fiji in the long term.

Endnotes

CHAPTER 1: MAYHEM AND MUTINY

1 This section draws heavily on an earlier essay: R. Robertson, 'A House Built on Sand', *Time* magazine, Sydney, 24 July 2000, p.16.

2 *Age*, Melbourne, 23 May 2000, p.14.

3 In April 2001 Mara somewhat belatedly revealed that he found Rabuka's 1987 coups 'disgusting'. He added that in his seven years in government, Rabuka showed that 'he couldn't run an office' (*Closeup* interview with Mara, Fiji TV, unofficial transcript on pcgovt.org.fj (hereafter *coalition*), 29 April 2001. Rabuka responded: 'He is an angry and jealous old man', *fijilive.com* (hereafter *fijilive*), 2 July 2001.

4 David Robie, 'Coup Coup Land: The Press and the Putsch in Fiji', paper to the Journalism Education Association Conference, Queensland, 5–8 December 2000, p.9.

5 Michael Field, 'Farewell to Coup Coup Land', *Fiji Times* (*FT*), Suva, 8 August 2000, p.7.

6 *Fijilive*, 23 October 2000; 17 February 2001; *The Review: The News and Business Magazine of Fiji* (hereafter *Review*), Suva, August 2000, pp.19–20; Joseph Veramu, Fiji Community Education Association president, *scoop.co.nz* (a New Zealand parliamentary journalism web service, hereafter *scoop*), 5 February 2001.

7   *coalition,* 1 May 2001.

8   Jon Fraenkel (*Review*, June 1999, p.44) argues that first past the post voting would have given Labour three seats less and the SVT nine more seats. Under proportional representation Labour would have only got 24 seats, the routed National Federation Party 10, and the SVT 15. The rival Fijian parties would have accumulated 19 seats (14 under first past the post) instead of the 20 they did.

9   Militoni Leweniqila, see Jone Dakuvula, 'Defending George Speight', *coalition*, 2 November 2000.

10   *coalition,* 2 November 2000.

11   Liu Muri, 'Truth about the Preferential Voting System', *fijilive*, 10 December 2000.

12   *Review*, February 2000, p.14.

13   Dakuvula, *coalition*, 2 November 2000.

14   John Wilson, 'A Document for the People', *FT,* Suva, 13 October 2000, pp.8-9.

15   Rowan Callick, *Australian Financial Review*, Sydney, 15 July 2000.

16   *Review*, December 1999, p.28.

17   *FT*, 20 December 1999, p.3.

18   *coalition*, 29 April 2001.

19   Jone Dakuvula, *coalition*, 2 November 2000; *FT*, 1 April 2000, p.1.

20   Dakuvula claims that the NLTB has no interest in resettling evicted farmers, ensuring that farming continues on vacated land, or that *mataqalis* maintain their present levels of rental income. 'Just getting the land back to the Fijians is the objective...,' Jone Dakuvula, 'More Land Gossip from the Grassroots', Citizens Constitutional Forum, *ccf.org.fj*, 2 May 2001. Some Coalition ministers believe that the NLTB hatched the coup in conjunction with Fijian Holdings Ltd. They also believe that a senior executive of FHL was to have provided the public face for the coup, but got cold feet. George Speight was brought in instead (*coalition*, 18 May 2001).

21   Minister for National Planning, Ganesh Chand, *FT,* 21 December 1999, p.3.

22   The wives of Tora and Savua are half sisters (*FT*, 29 April 2000, p.1).

23   See comments of Dr Anirudh Singh (*FT,* 4 May 2000, p.6), constitutional lawyer Yash Ghai on the Social Justice and Affirmative Action Bill, and journalist Tamarisi Digitaki ('Dangerous Tinkering', *Review*, April 2000, p.17).

24   *FT*, 10 February 2000, p.3.

25 *FT,* 4 May 2000, p.6.

26 This theory was put forward by FAP's Viliame Volavola, the Coalition's Minister of Urban Development and Housing (*FT,* 23 May 2000) and Australian High Commissioner Sue Boyd (*New Zealand Herald Online* [hereafter *NZH*], 21 August 2000). Interim Prime Minister Lai Qarase also claimed to know of the 'rumblings within the Coalition' and thought that the planned vote of no confidence had a good chance of succeeding (*Review*, August 2000, p.11). But some Labour Party officials denied the rumour (*FT,* 23 August 2000, p.3).

27 *Review*, June 2000, p.11.

28 'The Truth', *Fiji Sun*, Suva, 14 September 2000.

29 Commander Bainimarama contests this interpretation, which is based on the statements of the CRWU's Tikotani below. He believes that Duvuloco and his marchers had no foreknowledge of the coup. 'Speight's group simply took advantage of that march.' (Shailendra Singh, 'The Thin Line', *Review*, December 2000, p.14). Other writers have speculated that it was Duvuloco's unexpected arrival on the scene that prevented the coup going ahead as planned.

30 After Ligairi left the CRWU, the unit was placed under the command of Rabuka's 1987 co-conspirator, Lt Col Naivaluvua. In 1998 the unit was renamed the First Meridian Squadron and placed under the command of Penaia Baleinamau.

31 Interview with Jana Wendt, *Dateline,* SBS, 31 May 2000; see also Shailendra Singh, 'A disaster waiting to happen', *Review*, December 2000, pp.14–15.

32 Indeed Mara alleges that Ligairi met with Jioji Konrote (Rabuka's former Deputy Commander and now Permanent Secretary for Home Affairs) and Savua that same day (Tuesday 16 May; *coalition*, 29 April 2001). If true this would seem to suggest that the coup was hatched by members of the CRWU during the previous weekend anniversary. But Lt Col Viliame Seruvakula, commanding officer of the Third Fiji Regiment, claims Speight was recruited three weeks earlier (interview, Fiji TV, reported *coalition*, 22 April 2001). He also claims to have known in advance of the coup and had planned to pre-empt it (*coalition*, 11 April 2001). Mara's secretary, Jo Browne, tells a different tale, one that also hints at last minute organisation. One day before the coup, one of the rebels came to him to receive a written undertaking that Mara

would receive the petition. 'This for me is the same guy who links all the different parties together', he says (*fijilive*, 3 June 2001).

33 Christopher Dore, 'How Fiji talked itself into a coup', *The Australian*, 24–25 June 2000, p.14. See also 'How the Coup was Staged', *Review*, June 2000, pp.10–12.

34 As a prominent politician and businessman, Ah Koy was an obvious target for coup conspiracies. In the past he has been accused of bankrolling Rabuka's coup. On this occasion his closeness to the Speight family inevitably raised the same accusations. Like many business people, he did not prosper under Labour. His computer firm, Datec, allegedly lost a $20 million government contract when the Coalition won office (*smh.com.au* [*Sydney Morning Herald*, hereafter *smh*], 8 July 2001) and reports during 2001 suggested that his business empire was in serious financial difficulties.

35 Speight's father was the illegitimate son of a Tailevu dairy farmer and was registered at birth in his mother's clan as Savenaca Tokainavo. He only started to use his father's name when he wanted a job at the Vatukoula gold mine. During colonial times, Fijians were sent down in the mines, but with a European name Speight was able to gain a much better-paid office job.

36 *Cyclone George*, 10 July 2000. One Fiji journalist wrote, 'Anyone who crossed Speight's path before he shot to international fame ... will recall a foul-mouthed *viavialevu* [upstart], trousers (not *sulu*) freshly pressed, mobile phone constantly in hand, and boasting of the next big deal' (Graham Davis, 'Is George dead man walking?', *FT*, 24 May 2001, p.17.

37 *Cyclone George*, 10 July 2000.

38 Interview with David Hardaker, *7.30 Report*, ABC, 12 June 2000.

39 *Cyclone George,* 10 July 2000.

40 ACP Rao, *scoop*, 29 September 2000. Mara also alleged that the police presence at the march had been suspiciously inadequate (Fiji TV transcript, *coalition*, 29 April 2001).

41 Timoci Caucau, *Wansolwara*, University of the South Pacific (USP), Suva, June 2000, p.5; Bainimarama (*Review*, December 2000, p.14) never thought that the demonstration might be a precursor to anything other than 'civil disturbances'.

42 *Review*, December 2000, p.15.

43 *Review*, June 2000, p.11; see also *FT*, 20 May 2000, p.9.

44 Mesake Koroi, 'Coup that almost succeeded … but', *fijilive*, 24 November 2000.

45 Interview with Di Martin, *Asia-Pacific*, Radio National, ABC, 17 August 2000. Tarakinikini denied Rabuka's allegation (*fijilive*, 19 August 2000). CRWU commander Lt Penaia Baleinamau was later charged by the military with authorising the release of weapons to the rebels (*coalition*, 9 May 2001). Extracts from CRWU affidavits published by the *Fiji Sun* claim that the military ordered them to hide their arms and ammunition, that they also provided the rebels food and transport, mobile phones, and made them apply for leave while at the Parliament 'providing security and guarding hostages' (*coalition*, 6 & 7 July 2001).

46 *scoop*, 18 August 2000.

47 ACP Subramani Rao, *scoop*, 29 September 2000; Poseci Bune, *fijilive*, 24 August 2000; *Review*, September 2000, p.12; and *Daily Post*, 13 December 2000. Speight was clearly considering his options at this point. When he met Browne at 13.30 he said 'they had nothing to do with the march or the military and were there to remove old MPs, that young people of Fiji had taken over, and there was no room for Mara and Browne in this government'(*fijilive*, 3 June 2001). Later an official inquiry by Chief Justice Timoci Tuivaga cleared Savua in October 2000. Its report has not been made public, but in May 2001 a letter from Speight to the Tuivaga inquiry became public. In it he denied that Savua had any involvement with the initial conspiracy (*fijilive*, 17 May 2001).

48 *fijilive*, 21 May 2000. *Daily Post* columnist Mesake Koroi alleges that Rabuka first asked Mara to make him Prime Minister and later military commander. Mara nearly gave in. Rabuka, he argues, desperately wanted to become the 'saviour of democracy' (*fijilive*, 10, 23 April 2001).

49 John Sharpham, *Rabuka of Fiji: The Authorised Biography of Major-General Sitiveni Rabuka*, Rockhampton: Central Queensland University Press, 2000.

50 *fijilive*, 21 May 2000. When Mara met Rabuka and Savua two days later on 21 May, he accused them both of complicity in the coup. 'You could see it on their faces,' he declared (*coalition*, 29 April 2001).

51 *FT*, 24 May 2000, p.9.

52 *Age*, 23 May 2000, p.14.

53 *fijilive*, 21 May 2000.

54 Economic consultant Navi Naisoro in *Cyclone George,* 10 July 2000.

55 *fijilive*, 21 May 2000.

56 Speight felt emboldened. The riots had bought him time. The leaders he expected might not have turned up, but many others had, and the rebel team now included former Fiji Intelligence Service chief Metuisela Mua, Duvuloco, former military lawyer Lt Col Tevita Bukarau, journalist Joe Nata, politician Simione Kaitani, and lawyer Ratu Rakuita Vakalalabure who assumed responsibility for the team's decrees. By mid afternoon on Day 1 of the crisis Speight was holding court with SVT officials like Kubuabola and Ah Koy. (Also present were Berenado Vunibobo, Paul Manueli, Ahmed Ali and Cakanauto. *Age,* 23 May 2000, p.1; *Pacnews,* 26 May 2000). Indeed, the SVT's secretary-general (Jone Banuve, *fijilive,* 21 May 2000) told the media that his party and the four Fijian political parties were backing the coup and hoped to establish a government of Fijian National Unity. Also present at various times was the NLTB's general manager Maikau Qarikau, Tora, as well as FAP dissidents.

57 When Lt Col Seruvakula learned that Ligairi's coup plan involved Bainimarama's arrest, he despatched a platoon of 30 soldiers to meet Bainimarama at Nadi and escort him to Suva.

58 *FT,* 12 November 2000 (also *coalition,* 12 November 2000).

59 Tomasi Digitaki, 'In the Lion's Den', *Review,* July 2000.

60 Christopher Dore, 'Just another day in paradise', *Australian,* 27–28 May 2000, pp.21, 24.

61 Macuata chief Ratu Josefa Dimuri questioned Rabuka's wisdom in calling the GCC together and declared his support for an indigenous government. Some chiefs even threatened civil war if Mara ordered the military into the Parliament. Dimuri was supported by the Tui Navitilevu, Ratu Tevita Bolobolo and the Tui Labasa, Ratu Joeli Ritovu, *FT,* 22 May 2000, pp.3, 5.

62 Malcolm Brown, *Age,* 23 May 2000, p.1.

63 Tomasi Digitaki, 'In the Lion's Den', *Review,* July 2000.

64 *fijilive,* 23 May 2000.

65 *fijilive,* 25 May 2000.

66 Interview with Jana Wendt, *Dateline,* SBS, 31 May 2000. Later, on Radio Fiji, Rabuka also conceded that he had been wrong to overthrow his senior officers in 1987. 'I served with a few commanders when I was in the army and

I can't say that I totally agreed with their methods of leadership, but that didn't give me the right to try and oust them.' (*fijilive*, 7 November 2000).

67 Soldiers were promised cash and packages of benefits if they joined the rebels. Faxes sent from the parliamentary complex told soldiers not to support Bainimarama as he was a naval man. They also declared that it was their duty to support indigenous rights (*FT*, 31 May 2000, p.4; 31 March 2001, p.10).

68 Mary-Louise O'Callaghan ('Rabuka legacy rule by the gun', *Australian*, 26 May 2000, p.1) commented: 'For all his recent leadership on the issue of the new constitution and a multiracial future for Fiji, Rabuka could not undo the precedent Speight and those backing him seized upon to justify their actions and seek amnesty.' Speight's 'no other way' mimicked Rabuka's own justification for his 1987 coups and the title of his first biography.

69 *fijilive*, 27 May 2000.

70 President's press conference, *fijilive*, 28 May 2000.

71 *FT,* 29 May 2000, p.1.

72 *fijilive*, 28 May 2000.

73 Joseva Savua and Jone Banuve made the threats. The newsreader was Virisila Buadromo; see Brian Woodley, 'Courage under fire', the *Australian 'Media'* magazine, 8–14 June 2000, pp.6–7.

74 *Fiji Sun*, 31 May 2000, p.11.

75 Australian Foreign Minister Alexander Downer revealed that Speight had threatened that Adi Koila would be the first hostage shot if the army stormed Parliament; *Australian*, 30 May 200, p.1.

76 Browne interview, *fijilive*, 1 May 2001; Mesake Koroi, *fijilive*, 6 May 2001.

77 *Australian*, 30 May 2000, p.8.

78 *coalition*, 29 April 2001. In fact the naval vessel *Kiro* soon moved away from Suva harbour after a rebel-controlled boat allegedly threatened it.

79 *The Muanikau Accord*, 9 July 2000, Article I.

80 *FT*, 21 February 2001. *Daily Post* journalist Mesake Koroi alleges that the Military Council only wanted to suspend the Constitution until the parliamentary stand-off was resolved and that Rabuka advised it to abrogate the Constitution instead (*fijilive*, 23 April 2001).

81 *coalition*, (Mara) 29 April 2001; (Browne) 1 May 2001.

82 *FT*, 1 September 2000, p.6.

83   *bbc.co.uk* (hereafter *bbc*), 31 May 2000.

84   *FT*, 2 June 2000, p.2.

85   Testimony of Col Jeremai Waqanisau, later President Iloilo's private secretary, and allegedly the leader of the delegation that presented Speight a *tabua*,
a traditional whale's tooth offering (*scoop*, 19 April 2001). The delegation
allegedly included two bus loads of soldiers including Savenaca Draunidalo,
Alfred Tuatoko, Ulaisi Vatu, Maciu Cerewale, Tarakinikini, and Etuweni Caucau.
The *Fiji Sun* later published extracts from CRWU affidavits claiming that the
delegation told the rebels in Parliament that the army had asked Mara to step
aside, had abrogated the Constitution, supported Speight or the coup's objectives, and now wanted the rebels to disperse and allow the military to take
over (*coalition*, 7 July 2001).

86   Interview with Maxine McKew, *7.30 Report*, ABC, 1 June 2000.

87   Murray Mottram, 'Speight meets his match', *Age*, 5 June 2000, p.15.

88   *Australian*, 6 June 2000, p.9.

89   Chen Young, *FT*, 16 April 2001, p.5. Justices Scott and Fatiaki were alleged
to have assisted Tuivaga.

90   *Age*, 9 June 2000, p.11.

91   Interview with David Hardaker, *7.30 Report*, ABC, 12 June 2000.

92   Jon Fraenkel, 'A flawed transition from village rulers', *Australian*, 14 June
2000, p.10.

93   The Tui Namosi, Ratu Suliano Matanitobua, *FT*, 16 June 2000, p.1.

94   Rabuka was also under fire. Both his GCC deputy chairperson, Adi Litia
Cakobau, and the rebel Silatolu demanded his resignation for manipulating
the Council when it last met. He was also persona non grata with Ligairi,
who refused to allow him back into Parliament. Why had he abandoned his
1987 goals? Why had he frustrated the rebels ever since May 19? Ligairi asked
(*fijilive*, 24, 28 June 2000).

95   *Australian* , 26 June 2000, p.8.

96   *Australian*, 27 June 2000, p.9.

97   *Australian,* 3 July 2000, p.12.

98   *Australian*, 29 June 2000, p.10.

99   *FT*, 7 July 2000, p.1.

100   *fijilive,* 4 July 2000.

101   SBS, 5 July 2000.

102   *FT*, 1 September 2000, p.1.

103   In a letter to the *Fiji Times*, Timoci Gaunavinaka from Naitasiri defended the
rebels. The British took Fijian lands by means of guns but were never labelled
terrorists, he argued. Rabuka criticised Speight for his coup and blamed Fijians
for his party's fall from grace but he never mentioned its $210 million fraud
under his leadership. The army condemned power cuts to Suva but proposed
the same for Parliament. He added: 'I have visited Parliament a few times
and have slept and ate with these so-called thugs and terrorists. One thing I
know for certain, they are not hypocrites.' *FT*, 16 July 2000, p.6.

104   *fijilive*, 7 July 2000.

105   Christopher Dore, 'Fiji: Beer, grog, golf and girls?' *Australian,* 15–16 July
2000, pp.1, 13.

106   *FT*, 11 July 2000, p.3.

107   *Australian*, 13 July 2000, p.7.

108   Australian clothing manufacturer Mark Halabe later acknowledged that he
contributed $50,000 towards the transportation costs of the *Bose ni Turaga*.
Many businessmen obviously contributed towards the cost of providing food,
transport and mobile phone services to the rebels during the 70-day ordeal.
Halabe was the first to acknowledge his role. He regarded Speight as a friend
(Andrew West, Aussie 'paid coup leader', *smh*, 8 July 2001.

109   *fijilive,* 13 July 2000.

110   *Age*, 17 July 2000, p.3.

111   Paul Daley, 'Speight savours the day with tea and cake', *Age*, 15 July 2000.

112   Malcolm Brown, 'Speight warns of another coup', *smh*, 17 July 2000.

113   Speight's supporters in Qarase's administration included Tora, Takiveikata, Adi
Finau Tabakaucoro, Simione Kaitani, Silatolu, and Kubuabola; SBS, 19 July
2000; *smh*, 19 July 2000.

114   *FT*, 21 July 2000, p.2.

115   The rebels vented their anger on vehicles in the parliamentary compound,
stopping the destruction only when they learned that the swearing-in had
been postponed. As six busloads of rebels departed for Kalabu, they left
behind the charred remains of torched vehicles and a shattered parliamentary complex. Condoms and women's under-garments lay strewn around
offices. The parliamentary library lay in ruins, victim of a futile attempt to
find a secret tunnel to the President's residence. But the wanton destruction

was not over yet. As they passed through the Laqere market, the rebels looted
it of fish and root crops (*fijilive*, 26 July 2000).

116   Savua and Takiveikata claimed to be mediating. The talks continued at the
Nabua Police Station on the Friday (*FT*, 21 July 2000, p.5).

117   *FT*, 25 July 2000, p.1. Adi Samanunu's first foray into politics had been less
than auspicious. The wife of a former British army officer, she had successfully contested the 1994 election as an SVT candidate, although her British
citizenship disqualified her. She resigned one year later, technically state-
less, because the drafters of the 1990 Constitution had omitted to allow a
mechanism by which former citizens could regain citizenship (see Robert
T. Robertson, *Multiculturalism & Reconciliation in an Indulgent Republic: Fiji
after the Coups 1987–1998*, Suva: Fiji Institute of Applied Studies, 1998,
pp.147–148).

118   Rumours suggested Savua sought a ministry in the new Cabinet line-up (*fijilive*,
27 July 2000, p.1).

119   These are Tarakinikini's observations on the meeting which took place on the
same day the French Concorde crashed in Paris (*smh*, 27 July 2000).

120   Electricity was still in short supply; rebels continued to hold Monasavu and
its power generation facilities. In the west, members of the deposed government and local chiefs again threatened to establish a breakaway state. The
Chief Magistrate, Salesi Temo, acquitted a rebel charged with shooting two
soldiers and a journalist on 27 May. In Suva trade unions and civic organisations planned a series of demonstrations demanding the reinstatement of
Fiji's democratically elected government. On Saturday morning a small
number of rebels attempted to seize the Rewa Bridge along the vital
Suva–Nausori corridor. Rebels also attacked a village outside Savusavu. In
Suva the 'dogs of war' plundered neighbourhoods around Kalabu for food
and cash.

121   Tony Parkinson, 'The rebels had military chief in their sights', *Age*, 3 November
2000; see also a Radio Fiji Report, *Pacific Media Watch*, Suva, 20 October
2000.

122   Amidst the alarm, Qarase's administration released a mini budget. 'We are a
sovereign country', he reminded Fiji's neighbours. 'We are capable of solving
our own problems. We don't need to be told what is the right form or the
right way of doing things' (*FT*, 28 July 2000, p.13).

123 Tarakinikini continued to be the subject of numerous allegations linking him to both the coup plotters or to the mutineers (*coalition*, 15 June 2001; 6 July 2001).

124 *FT*, 12 November 2000; *Review*, December 2000, p.15.

125 The Tui Ba, Adi Senimili Cagilabu and the chair of the Kadavu Provincial Council, Ratu Jo Nawalowalo; *FT*, 10 November 2000, p.8.

126 *Age*, 3 November 2000.

127 *fijilive*, 3 November 2000.

128 Sophie Foster Hildebrand, 'Strangers in the camp', *FT*, 6 November 2000, p.7.

129 Singh, *Review*, December 2000, p.12; *scoop*, 31 October 2000.

130 Singh, *Review*, December 2000, p.15.

131 Early reports suggested some rebels died during the counter offensive, but immediately after the failed mutiny the wife of one dead soldier claimed that her husband – who had not participated in the mutiny – had been taken to the barracks after the event. In March 2001 the police announced they were investigating the five deaths as murder. All the dead soldiers had been arrested outside the barracks during the mutiny and kept at the Central Police Station in Suva. They were later taken to the Nabua barracks where they died (*FT*, 26 March 2001, p.1).

132 Some reports also suggested a conspiracy involving senior officers and civilian rebel supporters, including a Naitasiri high chief; *FT*, 9 November 2000, p.1; *coalition*, 12 November 2000; Singh, *Review*, December 2000, p.15.

133 *fijilive*, 7 November 2000.

134 *Review*, October–November 2000, p.17.

135 *fijilive*, 16 October 2000.

136 *FT*, 2 December 2000, p.9.

137 In May 2001 Qarase finally released a Blueprint for Fijian Education, detailing a much needed $8.4 million injection of capital into Fijian educational infrastructure. But it was a technocratic response only, and did nothing to address the concerns of the Education Commission, whose report remained hidden from public scrutiny.

138 *FT*, 12 November 2000 (see also *coalition*, 12 November 2000).

139 *FT*, 26 February 2001, p.3.

140 *FT*, 8 December 2000, p.2.

141 Mark Chippendale, 'Qarase sees a future of affirmative action', *smh*, 19 February
     2001.

142 *fijilive*, 16 November 2000.

143 *fijilive*, 8 November 2000.

144 *scoop*, 27 November 2000.

145 *FT*, 14 December 2000, p.7.

146 *FT*, 15 January 2001.

147 *scoop*, 20 December 2000.

148 *FT*, 1 September 2000, p.7.

149 *fijilive*, 27 April 2001.

150 *FT*, 4 May 2001, p.4.

151 Charles Sampford, 'Dare to call it treason', *Overhere.com*, May 2001.

152 Singh, *Review*, December 2000, p.15. In Lautoka Justice Anthony Gates first
     declared the abrogation of the Constitution illegal, condemned the actions of
     senior judges that assisted the military commit illegal acts, and resisted the
     Chief Justice's efforts to transfer other constitutional cases to Suva.

153 *FT*, 1 September 2000, p.7.

154 *fijilive*, 3 May 2001.

155 *fijilive*, 27 April 2001.

156 *coalition*, 18 May 2001.

157 *fijilive*, 21 May 2001.

158 *FT*, 15 December 2000, p.7. Indeed the President's secretary had advised the
     army against the path it took. 'In fact they actually shot themselves in the
     foot', Browne argues, 'because what they did they could have done under the
     authority of [the President]'. By removing the President, they removed his
     authority, and made their own acts illegal (*fijilive*, 3 June 2001).

159 The Chief Justice, already under fire for seeking to transfer constitutional
     cases from Lautoka to Suva, had earlier assured judges that any judge involved
     in advising the former President or the military would not hear cases chal-
     lenging the consequences of their advice. But when the CCF case came before
     Justice Daniel Fatiaki, allegedly a co-adviser along with Justice Scott, he
     initially refused to disqualify himself. Later he stood down and Justice Scott
     assumed the case (*fijilive*, 15 May 2001).

160 *fijilive*, 14 May 2001; 23 April 2001.

161 *fijilive*, 18 July 2001.

CHAPTER 2: THE QUEST FOR FIJIAN PARAMOUNTCY

1 *FT*, 1 April 1999, p.1.

2 K.L. Gillion, *Fiji's Indian Migrants: A History to the End of Indenture in 1920*, Melbourne, Oxford University Press, 1962, p.7.

3 P. France, *The Charter of the Land: Custom and Colonisation in Fiji*, Melbourne, Oxford University Press, 1969, p.108.

4 Paul Geraghty, *Island Business*, February 1992, p.19.

5 Taniela Tabu, *FT*, 9 October 1993, p.1.

6 The Tui Yale, Ratu Mosese Builomaloma, *FT*, 14 October 1994, p.1.

7 *FT,* 2 January 1995, p.6.

8 *Daily Post*, 8 October 1993, p.2.

9 Gillion, *Fiji's Indian Migrants,* p.100.

10 Gillion, op cit, p.74.

11 For a fuller discussion see Sutherland, *Beyond the Politics of Race, An Alternative History of Fiji to 1992*, Canberra, Australian National University, 1992, pp.62–79.

12 *Fiji Legislative Council Debates*, Suva, 1946, p.163.

13 *Fiji Legislative Council Debates*, p.170.

14 *Fiji Legislative Council Debates,* p.178.

15 Sutherland, op cit, p.136.

16 R.V. Cole, S. Levine and A.V. Matahau, *The Fijian Provincial Administration: A Review*, Suva, Parliamentary Paper 55, 1985.

17 Robert Norton, *Race and Politics in Fiji*, St Lucia, Queensland University Press, 1972, p.223.

18 O. Spate, *The Fijian People: Economic Problems and Prospects,* Suva, Legislative Council Paper 13, 1959, p.5.

19 Burns et al, 1960, p.31.

20 C.S. Belshaw, *Under the Ivi Tree: Society and Economic Growth in Rural Fiji*, London, Routledge and Kegan Paul, 1964, p.236.

21 *FT*, 28 June 1965.

22 Ali, 1977, p.194.

23 Ali, p.190.

24 *Islands Business*, Sept 1987. See also Lal, 1989, p.6

25 *South Pacific Forum*, Suva, July 1985, pp.70–81.

CHAPTER 3

1   *Fiji Poverty Report*, Suva, UN Development Program, 1996.

2   Sutherland, *Beyond the Politics of Race*, p.159.

3   Jacqui Leckie, 'State Coercion and Public Sector Unionism in Post-Coup Fiji', *NZ Journal of Industrial Relations,* 16, 1991, pp.49–71.

4   *fijilive*, 1 December 2000.

5   *Review*, May 1996, p.15.

6   *Fiji Sun*, 14 July 2000.

7   This is described fully in William Sutherland, 'Global Imperatives and Economic Reform in the Pacific Island States', *Development and Change*, Oxford, Blackwell Publishers, 31 (2: March 2000), pp.459–480.

8   Steven Ratuva, 'Addressing Inequality? Economic affirmative action and communal capitalism in post-coup Fiji', in A. Haroon Akram-Lodhi, *Confronting Fiji Futures*, Canberra, Asia Pacific Press, 2000, p.232.

9   Ratuva, pp.230–231.

10   Ratuva, p.231.

11   Ratuva, p.233.

12   Ratuva, pp.232–233.

13   Ratuva, p.239.

14   Ratuva, pp.242–243.

15   Ratuva, pp.241–245.

16   Ratuva, p.244.

17   Liu Muri, 'Fiji Holdings Ltd and the Blueprint', *fijilive*, 14 January 2001.

18   Ratuva, pp.240–241, 244; Scott MacWilliam, 'Back to Back They Faced Each Other: Indigenous Capital in Fiji', paper delivered to ANU seminar, Canberra, 2000, p.11.

19   *fijilive*, 1 November 2000.

20   MacWilliam, p.18.

21   Ratuva, pp.245–246; see also 'Fijian Holdings Ltd: Why an independent inquiry is needed', *coalition*, 24 January 2001.

22   Sutherland, *Beyond the Politics of Race*, p.145.

23   ibid, p.146.

24   ibid, p.147.

25 Sutherland, 'The problematics of reform and the "Fijian" question', in Akram-Lodhi, *Confronting Fiji Futures*, p.212.

26 Ratuva, p.235.

27 Robert T. Robertson, *Multiculturalism and Reconciliation in an Indulgent Republic. Fiji after the Coups: 1987–1998*, Suva, Fiji Institute of Applied Studies, 1998, p.141.

28 Ratuva, p.237.

29 *Review*, January 1995, pp.12, 15.

30 Robertson, op cit, pp.140–141.

31 *Blueprint for the Protection of Fijian & Rotuman Rights and Interests, and the Advancement of their Development* (hereafter referred to as *Blueprint for Fijian Development*), presentation to the Great Council of Chiefs by the Interim Prime Minister, Mr Laisenia Qarase, 13 July 2000, at *fijilive*, 14 July 2000.

32 Sutherland, 'The problematics of reform', pp.215-218.

33 *Review*, May 1995, pp.28–29.

34 *Review,* May 1995, p.29.

35 *Review*, August 1995, p.38.

36 Ratuva, p.237.

37 *FT*, 11 October 1995, p.14.

38 Sutherland, *Beyond the Politics of Race*, p.187.

39 ibid, pp.201–202; Robertson, op cit, p.59.

40 Statement by the People's Coalition Government to the Africa–Caribbean–Pacific Fact-Finding Mission on the Fiji Crisis, *coalition*, 6 August 2000.

41 *Daily Post*, 30 August 2000.

42 *FT*, 26 November 2000.

43 *Daily Post*, 30 November 2000.

44 ibid.

CHAPTER 4

1 'Resolving the Political Crisis in Fiji', *Review*, October–November 2000.

2 *FT*, 26 August 2000, p.2.

3 *fijilive*, 11 August 2000.

4   *FT,* 23 September 2000, p.2.

5   Mary-Louise O'Callaghan, 'The Indian farmer who stood up for Fiji's democracy', *Australian*, 3–4 March 2001, p.11.

6   ibid.

7   *FT,* 24 June 1997, p.7.

8   *FT,* 7 June 1997, pp.1, 4.

9   *Fijilive,* 29 July 1999.

10 Brij Lal, 'Of Speights and Hansons and the Fiji Crisis', *FT,* 31 August 2000, p.7.

11 *FT,* 26 August 2000, p.2.

12 'Resolving the Political Crisis in Fiji', *Review*, October–November 2000.

13 *FT,* 12 October 2000, pp.28–29.

14 Robert Wolfgramm, 'Fiji seeks its own way', *Age*, 19 July 2000; also published in the *Daily Post,* 15 July 2000, as 'Why democracy has failed'.

15 *scoop*, 17 July 2000.

16 John Davies, 'On the Source of Inter-Ethnic Conflict in Fiji', p.13.

17 Greg Sheridan, 'Melanesia: modern one day, primitive the next', *Australian*, 2 June 2000, p.11.

18 *fijilive*, 9 December 2000.

19 Submission to the Constitutional Review Commission, *FT,* 13 July 1995, p.5.

20 *Weekender*, Suva, 25 June 1993, p.11.

21 *Australian*, 14 June 2000, p.10.

22 *FT*, 16 September 2000, p.12.

23 *FT*, 21 October 2000, p.10.

24 Sione Masina, 'Rebels, Terrorists and Thugs', *Tonga Online*, 25 August 2000.

25 *NZ Herald Online*, 26 June 2000.

26 *Review*, December 2000, p.16.

27 *FT,* 12 February 2001, p.1.

28 Steven Ratuva, 'Addressing inequality', *Confronting Fiji Futures*, pp.232–233.

29 'The Chosen One', *Review*, August 2000, p.11.

30 Ratuva, 'Addressing inequality', pp.237–238.

31 Helen Tavoa (a consultant with the Education Commission), 'Education lessens poverty', *FT*, 30 November 2000, p.7.

32 Pio Rokosuka, 'When will Fijians ever learn', *FT*, 14 July 2000, p.7.

33 *FT,* 16 March 2001, p.7.

34 *Islands Business*, February 1994, p.43.

35 *Review*, November 1996, p.25.
36 Simione Durutalo, *FT*, 16 August 1991, p.1.
37 *fijilive*, 25 July 2001.
38 *FT,* 15 December 2000, p.7.
39 Victor Lal, 'The threat of separation in western and northern Fiji and some legal aspects', *fijilive*, 20 July 2000.
40 Sir Paul Reeves, Tomasi Vakatora, Brij Lal, *The Fiji Islands: Towards a United Future*, Suva, Report of the Fuji Constitutional Review Commission, 1996, p.xix.

Index